# Spiritual Mentoring

# Spiritual Mentoring

GUIDING PEOPLE THROUGH
SPIRITUAL EXERCISES
TO LIFE DECISIONS

## Tad Dunne

HarperSanFrancisco
*A Division of* HarperCollins*Publishers*

FIRST EDITION

**Library of Congress Cataloging-in-Publication Data**

Dunne, Tad, 1938–
    Spiritual mentoring : guiding people through spiritual exer-
cises to life decisions / Tad Dunne.—1st ed.
        p.    cm.
    ISBN 0-06-062109-5 (alk. paper)
    1. Spiritual direction.  2. Ignatius, of Loyola, Saint, 1491–
1556. Exercitia spiritualia.  I. Title.
    BX2350.7.D85   1991
253.5′3—dc20                                                    90-55343
                                                                        CIP


91 92 93 94 95 MART 10 9 8 7 6 5 4 3 2 1

This edition is printed on acid-free paper that meets the American
National Standards Institute Z39.48 Standard.

*To Dorothy*

# Contents

Acknowledgments     *xi*
Introduction     *xiii*

**One.  Retreat: Realizing Our Baptism**     *1*

1. Realizing Our Baptism     *2*
2. The Grammar of Retreat     *4*
3. A Definition of "Retreat"     *7*
4. "God"     *10*

**Two.  Spiritual Praxis**     *14*

1. Practice versus Praxis     *14*
2. Discernment of Spirits     *16*
3. Discernment of Stories     *19*
4. Praxis and Tradition     *22*
5. Praxis and Community     *24*
6. Technique     *26*
7. Liberation Praxis     *28*
8. The Circle of Praxis     *30*

**Three.  Our Primary Relationship: God**     *32*

1. The Double Question of God     *33*
2. God's Double Response     *37*
3. Shared Life with God     *43*
4. The Broken Relationship     *46*
5. The Symbol "Kingdom of God"     *49*
6. The Reign of God in History     *53*

**Four.   The Image of History**   *60*

   1. A Process Image   *61*
   2. Four Ways to Make Sense   *63*
   3. Four Process Images   *66*
   4. History of the Dialectical Image   *74*
   5. Conversion of the Imagination   *78*


**Five.   The Praxis of Noticing**   *84*

   1. Principles   *84*
   2. What to Notice   *91*
   3. Noticing Consolation and Desolation   *96*


**Six.   The Praxis of Meditation**   *104*

   1. The History of Meditation   *104*
   2. The New Questions   *111*
   3. Meditation as Understanding
      the Concrete Meaning of Love   *116*
   4. The Purpose of Meditation   *120*


**Seven.   The Praxis of Contemplation**   *125*

   1. A Mixed Legacy   *125*
   2. A Definition   *127*
   3. Real Assent   *133*
   4. The Dynamics of Real Assent   *139*
   5. The Purpose of Contemplation   *142*
   6. The Pinnacle of Contemplation   *144*


**Eight.   The Praxis of Deliberation**   *147*

   1. Decision: The Link between Spirit
      and History   *148*
   2. Feelings: Prelude to a Choice   *150*
   3. The Ambiguity of Feelings   *152*

4. Conscience: Arbiter of Values    *153*
5. The Limits of Conscience    *157*
6. Being in Love    *161*
7. The Decision: Realizing One's Conversion    *167*
8. The Decision: A Collaborative Action    *170*
9. Integrating the Choice into One's Life    *172*

**Appendix: Psychoanalysis, Counseling, Spiritual Mentoring**    *177*

**Notes**    *185*

**Index of Subjects and Names**    *193*

# Acknowledgments

This work is the fruit of many years teaching, conversing, and spiritual mentoring. While it is difficult to point out specific debts of gratitude, I want the reader to know the sources of any wisdom that may be found here and to express some public appreciation for the support I received for my endeavor.

For teaching me that spirituality needs a theological foundation, my gratitude to Colin Maloney, and to Bernard Lonergan, S.J. For continuing and enthusiastic support of my intellectual endeavors, I am grateful to Tom Ewens, Howard Gray, S.J., May Ann Hinsdale, I.H.M., and Carla Mae Streeter, O.P. Finally, I am grateful to my wife, Dorothy Seebaldt. She has kept my theological musings in touch with everyday reality and taught me to see with my heart.

# Introduction

This volume, along with its companion, *Spiritual Exercises for Today: A Contemporary Presentation of the Classic Spiritual Exercises of Ignatius Loyola,* grew from a small project I undertook some years ago. I wanted to make the *Spiritual Exercises of St. Ignatius* more usable for men and women who face decisions in today's world. Their focus on the making of a crucial decision is what has made the *Exercises* so unique and so effective in the history of spirituality. My goal, like the goal of the *Exercises,* has been to produce a manual of spiritual calisthenics "for overcoming oneself and regulating one's life without being swayed by any inordinate attachment."[1] To put this in more contemporary terms, these are exercises for overcoming the compulsions and addictions that cloud good judgment and entangle a strategic, free choice.

However, while I have kept the goal, I have had to make some major revisions to the *Exercises* themselves, owing to the advances made since Ignatius composed them in the 1520s: advances in psychology, scriptural theology, historical criticism, socio-critical analysis, and the shift to method in philosophy. It is this last advance, the shift to method in philosophy,[2] that raised the hermeneutical questions of how human knowing and willing can be reliable. Hence it seemed necessary to write this second volume on the elements of discretion that lie behind every decision.

Also, I have reconceived the setting for a "retreat." As I explain more fully in *Spiritual Exercises for Today,* I consider any withdrawal from immediate concerns to assess and integrate one's life a "retreat." A "retreat" is not restricted to a week or a month of seclusion; it may happen in a single day or be extended over a number of months.

Furthermore, the "retreat director" or "spiritual director," as we shall see, does not really give directions. He or she is more of a spiritual *guide* or a "soul friend."[3] Therefore, for the sake of accuracy, I will generally use the term "spiritual mentor," although it may be used equivalently with the more common "spiritual director." In any case, the mentor may be any person willing and able to provide the psychological insight, the moral advice, and especially the spiritual guidance to someone making a serious decision. So let it be understood that by "spiritual mentor" I mean any spiritual companion whatsoever.

Some may object to my tampering with the original text of Ignatius, and, I must admit, I hesitated a long time before attempting any updated version. What tipped the scales for me was the realization that no wise mentor actually "follows the text." Even those who claim to give the exercises according to the book rely on a great deal more than the book. They use their *discretion* as a bridge between the old text and a flesh-and-blood retreatant trying to listen to the Spirit in a culture that would astound Ignatius.

The purpose of this volume is to help a mentor understand for himself or herself very precisely what this discretion means. There are no formulas or answers here. There are only pointers to the elements of wisdom, inviting the reader to understand his or her wisdom in more clear and explanatory terms. I might add that this discretion applies not only to using *Spiritual Exercises for Today* to direct the exercises but to any critique, emendation, or improvement on that book that a spiritual mentor feels necessary.

Both volumes emphasize experience before knowledge. The spiritual exercises in the companion book are designed not to teach about God but to help a person experience the aspirations, the hesitations, the hope, and the love that make a decision truly one's own. Likewise, the reflections on life choices in the present work draw the reader's attention to the inner events of noticing, understanding, realizing, believing, and loving that shape a decision rather than on any doctrines in a person's religious tradition.

Not that I discount doctrine. On the contrary, I believe that the only way to make an inherited doctrine meaningful in one's life is to repeat the experiences of those who first formulated the doctrine. In any case, I would rather help a Hindu love well than convince an egotist that Jesus is divine.

As a result, these two volumes can be used profitably by Christians of any denomination, even by people whose Christianity is merely nominal. I ask only that they make two "acknowledgments." The first acknowledgment is that Jesus of Nazareth and the historical events of his life constitute a "Word" of God without parallel. By "Word" I mean something that has been delivered purposefully by God and reveals God's intentions for humanity. By "without parallel" I mean that the life of Jesus is not one in a series of prophets, each with a particular charism. Rather, the meaning that Jesus incarnated is key to God's definitive Word in history. Any clarification of that Word coming later in history can never surpass it, only perfect it. Therefore, because that Word includes any historical events meaningfully connected to it, that Word is still being spoken. The Word of God is incomplete, and its perfection is an invitation from God to us, calling us to become part of God's Word through reconciliation with one another.

The second acknowledgment required to do these exercises is to accept the fact that God has given humans a share in the divine spirit of love. Within the human heart, within every human heart, there stirs a force of love that is God's own love. There is no need to think of that love as a person, nor to dote on the eternal relationships between this spirit and Christ and the one Christ called "Father." It is enough to regard it as an energy in consciousness and to call it by the common name "spirit." That force is often smothered by forces of selfishness and hatred within us and can seem never to have existed at all. Normally, however, I have used the capitalized form, "Spirit," simply to avoid confusion in talking about our spirits and the spirit of God, and not to sneak in some doctrinal presupposition about real distinctions in God.

The real sticking point of this second acknowledgment is the belief that we humans experience a divine love that enables us to interpret texts and to create and criticize authority structures with integrity. Here is where textual fundamentalists of all stripes, whether of the Bible or of the founding documents of a country or a community, will find these two volumes frightening, I suppose. For both the praxis of intelligent love and the spiritual exercises that I propose require an expectation that God can bring about new meanings for our times, meanings that do not contradict the old but go far beyond the original intentions of founders, including those of Jesus himself.

Having said that, I must also warn readers who do not hold the Christian creed that if they embark on these exercises, they will find themselves honoring God's Word and God's Spirit in ways very similar to the ways that drew fourth-century Christians to arrive at the alarming propositions found in the Nicene Creed and the decrees of Constantinople, that Jesus Christ is "God from God, Light from Light, True God from True God, one in being with the Father"; and that the Holy Spirit is the "Giver of life," who "with the Father and the Son is worshiped." If such propositional commitments make anyone hesitate, he or she might consider that it took three hundred years of prayer, reflection, and heated argument to arrive at these truths, truths whose meaning few Christians even today can explain very well.

# CHAPTER ONE

---

# Retreat:
# Realizing Our Baptism

Ignatius Loyola's *Spiritual Exercises* owe their extraordinary success for over three centuries not to the *idea* of a book of exercises but to the new *purpose* he gave the genre. During the fifteenth century, books of "spiritual exercises" were used to help a Christian's daily growth in familiarity with Christ Jesus and in the exercise of virtues. Ignatius, however, was interested more in assisting retreatants to make a single radical choice about life. A reading of his "Spiritual Exercises" would indicate that the radical choice he had in mind was the choice of a state of life—married or single, clerical or lay, for example—yet he actually used them more to help retreatants choose to root their present state of life in a spirituality that sought to imitate Christ even as far as actual poverty.

Today, of course, the idea that *any* state of life is permanent has evaporated in the light of the increased options available to most individuals and an unfortunate skepticism about permanent commitment to any way of life whatsoever. Also, the ascetical ideal of imitating Christ in poverty has been completely lost, even among dedicated Christians. In its place there has arisen a more general kind of "imitation" that lives out the sacrament of baptism as a dying and rising with Christ through the actual losses and failures that life delivers without the aid of asceticism.

## 1. REALIZING OUR BAPTISM

Even though the notion of a permanent state of life and the ideal of a literal imitation of Jesus are foreign to us, we can still retain Ignatius' core insight that a retreat should facilitate a radical choice about one's life. But we should understand that choice as not strictly about a state of life but as any concrete exercise of the paschal risk symbolized by baptism.

A choice, after all, is essentially not a change of circumstances; it is a change of *meaning*. Many people who have no options about occupation, living conditions, live-in relatives, or sudden losses still have a choice about the meaning they will give to their situations. Those who do enjoy several options, of course, have more control over their futures but face no less a crisis of the *meaning* they will give to that future.

Every change of meaning is a death, whether or not it brings new life. We die not only to destructive relationships but often enough to certain life-giving relationships in the hope that yet more life will result. That life may be the life of our child or spouse; it may be the life of the community or the church; or it may be our own life. All these forms of "death" realize our baptism, because baptism is not a sign of cleansing us from sin; rather, it is a sign of *dying* to a former self, of immersion into the most fearsome depth of earth (which, in biblical literature, is the sea, not the land) and a rising to a new life with wholly new meaning.

We can be called to die to our former selves in a number of different ways, but I believe we can classify our deaths into three basic kinds. Each kind represents very real crises and is apt material for a baptismal choice between life and death.

First there are the deaths that come with sheer growth or development. An eighteen-year-old moving away to college must say farewell to friends and family. A newlywed must die to the dating game. A couple in their forties may decide to quit punching time clocks and start their own business. For many people these developmental crises loom so large that they never really follow life's natural expansiveness but cling merely to what worked for them in the past. Others rush through any open door without a thought about the cost. In either case, the fear of death—in particular the fear of lost meanings—can prevent people from entering into life's natural baptisms.

Second, there are the deaths imposed on us by circumstances beyond our control. An accident kills one of our children. A corporation lays off the entire department where we work. Old age robs our sight or hearing. The meaning of life has already changed for us and we can never carry on as we once did.

Third, there are the deaths that come with *metanoia*—any complete change of heart or "conversion." A young man kicks a drug habit. A bachelor falls in love. A mother ends her bitter refusal to speak to an alienated daughter. Often the need to change our hearts—and the power to do it—lies beneath either a developmental change or a circumstantial change. A change of heart may involve turning away from some personal sinful habit or from a culture's sinful habit. In either case, we experience an inability to act sheerly on our own. We put our trust in God, hoping that there is life beyond any death. The only ultimate death is to stand before the deep water of baptism and refuse to die.

I have listed these various kinds of "death" to suggest not merely the types of choices one might contemplate during a retreat. I also want to suggest that we change our imagination about retreat itself. It is not a military "retreat" where we withdraw to regroup our forces; that image verges on a Pelagian self-sufficiency and overlooks the paschal mystery altogether. Nor is it a retreat aimed sheerly at a ritual reconciliation with God, as if we withdraw from ordinary life to touch base with God for a while, only to return to a mystery-less familiar life. Rather, a retreat is a dying and rising to the meaning of these many deaths in our familiar lives.

## 2. THE GRAMMAR OF RETREAT

Certainly "retreat" has meant different things to different people. What different people actually do "on retreat" will differ accordingly. Today, even business corporations offer "retreats" that have little connection to the religious tradition of retreating.

While we cannot copyright the definition of the word, we can and should ask what it means for ourselves. Without a clear idea of what we expect from a retreat, we lose our sense of what we want and how to get it. We return to our home and workplace more rested perhaps, and glad for the time away from everyday demands, but not always with a more effective direction in our lives. Even after an insightful homily, or a helpful conversation with a retreat mentor, the thrill of the moment can quickly evaporate, leaving only a dim memory. Our demeanor may change for a while, but our behavior remains the same.

This is a problem not only for a retreatant. Retreat house staffs spend months planning programs of reflection and prayer, spend thousands of dollars creating an atmosphere of quiet solemnity. Retreat mentors take courses on spiritual theology, communication skills and methods of prayer, and yet they soon discover they lack the criteria for determining when to use which skills.

How, for example, should a mentor decide whether to be more "directive" or more "indirective" with a given retreatant? How does a mentor know that one retreatant should use a "centering" prayer and another an imaginative contemplation of Christ? By default of objective criteria, mentors tend to rely exclusively on the methods they found useful for themselves.

I have found that one of the major roadblocks to a good retreat is *a failure to understand what kind of experience to anticipate*. Let me explain with an example.

It is commonplace to insist on the importance of knowing how much God loves us. But what kind of experience is that exactly? Is it ultimately a feeling? A raw belief? An insight? A vivid image? Without a clear understanding— and the ability to put it into words—of exactly the kind of experience "knowing the love of God" is, retreatants do not know what to look for. Consequently, they cannot intelligently participate in exercises designed to dispose them to "know God's love." Worse, when the mentors do not understand the experience clearly, they inadvertently devise exercises that in effect inhibit the experience they want to elicit.

It is humbling for retreat mentors to recall that the majority of profound spiritual experiences do not occur on retreat. Think of the elemental realizations that have opened your own eyes to the reality of God in the world. Think of the times when you felt so charged with a godly love that you began to act in surprisingly charitable ways. These inner revolutions can occur during a shower or while taking a trip. These are the experiences that any retreat ought to dispose a person for, whether or not they occur during that retreat.

To understand exactly the kind of experiences to anticipate for a person retreating, we need verbs. People say a retreat is for "getting closer to God" or "sorting out one's life." The trouble with "getting closer" and "sorting out" is that the actions they refer to are too ambiguous. And the reason they are ambiguous is that they are metaphors, not accurate denotations of specific, conscious acts. Compare, for example, the verbs drawn from consciousness in the left column with the verbs drawn from physical metaphors on the right:

| *Acts of Consciousness* | *Physical Metaphors* |
| --- | --- |
| notice | draw closer |
| understand | sacrifice |
| wonder | be filled with |
| realize | pursue |
| deliberate | journey |
| feel | heal |
| decide | rest |
| care for | resist |
| appreciate | give up |

The ˙physical metaphors in the right column have their place, certainly. They are very effective in discourse aimed at *encouraging* others. They give others the strong imagery and dramatic expression needed to continue on the path they have set for themselves. But they are no help at all if a person needs to change that path. For that, he or she needs to *understand* life in a new way and to *understand* how to go about changing the path.

The acts of consciousness in the left column are, in fact, technical terms. They may look commonplace, and to some extent people may disagree on their exact meanings, but in the chapters to follow I intend to give them precise definitions that will be useful in expressing what experiences are expected in a retreat. For now, my point is that both a mentor and a retreatant should express the aim of the retreat with a verb that represents an act of consciousness. These are the "graces" one seeks, and they should be named as such.

These verbs take objects, of course. I may want to appreciate God's goodness in giving me a certain friend. I may want to deliberate about taking a new job. I may simply want to feel genuine grief over my own sin. A good mentor will take some care to articulate both the verb and the object with a retreatant. This can take time, particularly when a retreatant comes with too large an agenda or, as often happens, has a more secret agenda than she or he is able to divulge. But even if it takes all seven days of a one-week retreat, it is well worth the effort to help a retreatant name the central, needed grace.

## 3. A DEFINITION OF "RETREAT"

If we are to understand the kind of experiences to anticipate in a retreat, we ought to define a "retreat" in terms of experiences we can name:

> *A retreat is a withdrawal from immediate concerns to assess and integrate one's relationships.*

Let me explain the elements of this definition. First, a retreat requires a *withdrawal from immediate concerns.* Many people come to retreat houses without ever leaving home, so to speak. Along with their suitcases, they carry in trunkloads of anxieties about bills to pay and relatives to phone. But there are others who have the power to pay quiet attention to their hearts whether or not they are engaged in any formal "prayer." The essential condition of a retreat is not a sequestered place and time but rather the personal ability to put one's "Things to Do" list on a shelf.

A retreat, therefore, can happen almost anyplace. Although a quiet setting away from home usually helps us to pull back from everyday life, what counts is that a person actually puts practical and personal worries out of mind, whether kneeling in a chapel or sipping coffee at the office. By "retreat," then, I will have in mind any of the following kinds of events:

- Five minutes alone getting perspective on a friendship.
- Asking someone for advice about whether to take a job.
- Writing journal reflections on your feelings.
- A "day of recollection" spent reading Scripture.
- A week at a retreat house "talking to God."

Keep these various kinds of retreat experiences in mind as you read further. I believe that keeping the focus on the *events expected* rather than on what words to use, what place to pray, or what behavior to hope for will be very helpful, not only for those who design and give retreats but also for any kind of spiritual mentors and pastoral counselors.

Also, the role of a retreat mentor can be the formal role whereby one person trained in the art helps another make a truly free response to God. Or it can be the informal role whereby one person acts as a sounding board for another who is making a decision. Again, while I will refer to the retreat (or spiritual) mentor often in this book, I am talking about anyone who performs the function of helping another freely respond to God. My hope is that in any case—including the spiritual mentoring one does for oneself—this book will clarify what that art is all about.

I have defined a retreat experience as a withdrawal from immediate concerns. Now, it takes some practice to learn how to still the inner voices of practicality. It is impossible to stop thinking about immediate matters without having something definite to turn our minds to. This brings us to another feature to notice about our definition. A retreat is not simply about "God" or about "me" or about "my work" or "my spouse." Fundamentally it is about my *relationships* to all of these.

After all, what makes us the persons we are is not some mysterious "self" hiding deep in our psyches. We are connected. We are persons-in-relation-in-history. We are born into a community with a heritage, and we speak with a "mother" tongue. We make friends, but friends make us too. Our profession is a statement of a specific kind of self we are in relationship to others. We look to God for forgiveness and strength. We die, and our loved ones carry on our hopes, sharing them with people we have never met. So the only way to make an intelligent commitment of a life is first by understanding these relationships as far as possible. These are what make up the life we are in fact leading.

Notice that a retreat experience ought to be about my actual relationships, not some ideal ones I wish I had. True, I can imagine better relationships, but I can never improve them unless I fearlessly admit what my relationships actually are. It is not enough to focus on God's general relation to the world or even on, say, Christ's attitude toward the poor. That is the work of theology; it is only a preparation for the essential work of a retreat. Nor is it enough to focus on how people in general deal with life. That is the work of psychology, sociology, and history. In fact, the very purpose of these sciences is ultimately to help me understand the concrete ways I relate to God, self, and neighbor.

What ought a retreat do for such relationships? First, it should *assess* them. By "assess" I am thinking of the times we evaluate our commitments to friends, to work, to country, to God, and even to ourselves. It is my experience that while many retreatants can surface some *feelings* about all these relationships, few muster the courage to coolly assess their value with real objectivity.

This is the real purpose of an "examination of conscience"—not a search for sins but an evaluation of one's relationships as they have become manifest in everyday behavior. It has been better referred to as an "examination of consciousness."[1] This is also the purpose of reading the Bible. We read in order to allow the historical manifestation of divine values to confront the historical manifestation of our own values. It is not enough to feel guilty or edified by what we read. The point is to reach a conviction about our relationships with a view to improving them.

A retreat should also *integrate* relationships. By "integrate" I mean that a retreat should help connect our relationships into a dynamic unity that will reveal itself in a new way of acting in the world. Obviously this integration may demand that we cut off certain harmful relationships, but not always. There are many instances where we ought to change our priorities about some relationships, and in practice this is sometimes even more difficult than dropping them outright.

It is important, however, to integrate the relationships we want to keep. This means not leaving any active relationships out of the picture, floating, as it were, making our lives an archipelago of unrelated concerns. In a healthy integration all subordinate relationships are enhanced by superior ones rather than being inhibited by them. For example, mature spouses not only nourish their mutual love; they also encourage each other to pursue rewarding hobbies, work, and friendships. Any need for secrecy, the first defense of a compartmentalized life, diminishes.

Such an integration does not happen fully during the retreat experience. We may see clearly how to reorder some commitments, but until we actually make the phone calls and write the letters—or stop making the phone calls and writing the letters—our relationships do not actually change. Integration, in other words, is realized only in action.

Finally, the retreat, as I have defined it, is essentially about the decision of an individual, not of a group. I will not discuss the topic of a communal decision made by spouses, a family, a church staff, a religious community. I hope that the insights into what individual freedom is about will be helpful to persons making a decision with others. But prior to such communal decisions, each party must assess and integrate the communal relationship on which the integrity of a group decision depends.


## 4. "GOD"

A word about the term *God*. I left the term out of the definition of a retreat. I did so because the word is a kind of metaphor and so is notoriously ambiguous. As the history of religions shows, not only have people disagreed on what "God" means, but those disagreements seem to have led to a rather godless hatred of one's neighbor. Even in our own personal lives we find that what "God" meant to us as children is quite different from what it means to us today. The word is unlike a name of someone we know well—"Martin Luther King." The word *God* is more like a tweezers to hold onto something we do not know well and yet have sufficient experience to ask questions about. In fact, we can find surprising agreement on the *experiences* that at least raise the question of God both in religions throughout history and in our personal religious development.

There are two ways in which the question of God occurs to us. One is the experience of hearing others, and the other is the experience of hearing our own hearts. People brought up in a religious family inherit a language, a worldview, and a lore about God. So questions arise, ranging from the naive question of what God looks like to the radical question of whether our belief is a belief in someone real. As a counterpoint to what we hear from others, we also feel a pull in our hearts toward appreciating or creating beauty always beyond what we have. We feel a natural inclination toward making sense of things, getting rid of illusions, and enhancing the world we share by good deeds. We experience a familiar love of a distant unknown, which as it draws us onward simultaneously beautifies and harmonizes the life we share with each other.

What we hear from others about God needs to be tested in what we experience ourselves. At the same time, what we experience ourselves needs to find a public language that other people can understand. So the outer word and the inner word go together. They complement each other. If we cannot find examples in our own experience that correspond to what the word of others says about God, their word remains meaningless for us. Likewise, if we cannot find common words in which to express what we have experienced, our understanding of our experience remains unformulated, untested, and ineffective.

It is very important to notice here that all religious expressions—all stories about God, all the art and music, all the Scripture, all the ideals encoded in laws and customs—are expressions of people's understanding of their inner experiences. That understanding is formulated in familiar words that may be more or less adequate to the experience. Over time a developing religious culture refines the meanings of the words and stories, dropping some expressions and borrowing others. But as children are born into that culture, there is the ongoing task of passing on the meaning of their religion. Beyond memorizing texts and learning pious behavior, new generations need to be taught the more difficult task of finding meaning in those texts and manners, something each person can only do by relating them to personal experience.

I would like, therefore, to abstain temporarily from the doctrines of God taught by our traditions. Instead I want to focus on the experiences of hearing others and of hearing our own hearts as the ever-fresh source of meaningfulness in the term *God.* I believe that anyone preparing to reassess and reintegrate some significant relationships ought to hold in abeyance the old doctrines and rituals and listen instead for when the inner word of the heart discovers its beloved in some outer word from one's culture and memory, from Scripture and song. Saint Augustine found the meaning of celibacy not in admonitions from the church or in any philosophical writings but in the living example of men and women. Only then did he see any meaning for his time from Christ's remark about eunuchs for the Kingdom.

In a retreat, therefore, we withdraw even from the formulas and doctrines of the religion we cherish. It is a retreat to the wellspring of religion, to the raw experience of life. Life, after all, is first. Life is God's hand-delivered invitation. Only in the lives we have do we discover the meanings of the lives of others, whether long deceased or at our side. Only in our own lives can we test religious claims made by others, and only here can we find any authority to make religious claims of our own.

Only in our own lives do we discover the real dimensions of the historical struggles of our community to make sense out of life, tolerating mistakes and forgiving sins as well as creating the wherewithal for the betterment of life. Even where we take on faith the lessons taught by others, we do so only to the degree that we love and trust them from the hearts we happen to have.

Finally, only in our own lives and the lives of those we love do we find God. We do not see God, yet we see the work of God all around us in the works of faith, hope, and charity. We see God's hand not only in our public and communal life but also in the interior, wordless life of each one's spirit. There, in the ever-present love for what delights the eye and ear, there in the constant yearning for more such delight, there in the inner Holy of Holies where we often dare not enter, there where our very longing for an absent Other can capitulate to despair, there is the Other present.

# CHAPTER TWO

# Spiritual Praxis

Because the title of this volume is *Spiritual Mentoring,* you might expect to find various practical techniques for guiding others here. But my purpose is not so much practical as prudential. It is less about spiritual recipes and more about spiritual wisdom. Yet even "prudence" or "wisdom" could connote a set of basic spiritual principles or a list of wise sayings from spiritual masters of the past—formulations for the would-be mentor to memorize, meditate upon, and apply in practice.

But you will find little of that here. Rather I hope to lead you to reflect on the workings of your own spirit and to discover there the true foundation for your own wisdom and prudence. For the purpose of referring to this inner work, and particularly to avoid the connotations of mere technique often associated with spiritual mentoring, I will use the recently revived term *praxis*. Let me explain what praxis means by contrasting it with "practice."

## 1. PRACTICE VERSUS PRAXIS

Practice deals with making or producing tangible, external effects. Praxis, by contrast, deals with how one conducts oneself, negotiates one's experiences and feelings. In other words, we engage in praxis before engaging in practice. Where practice is associated with practicality and know-how, praxis is associated with wisdom and discretion.

A book on the practice of retreat would deal with suggestions about what spiritual exercises to perform. It would offer guidelines on how to respond to different concrete experiences. It would present lore on prayer drawn from classical works on spirituality and from the experience of directing others. All of this can be found in *Spiritual Exercises for Today,* which is a manual or a resource book that a retreatant and a mentor use at their discretion.

Discretion, however, is not cheap. It cannot be learned by reading some other manual or even the spiritual classics. There are no "spiritual exercises" for improving one's discretion because, unlike most skills, it is impossible to practice on it before doing the real thing. We learn discretion only through making choices, accepting responsibility for their outcome, and reflecting on the quality of our deliberation. The learning of discretion is the work of praxis.

The praxis of retreat deals with the wisdom that decides which practical suggestions are appropriate in a given situation. It is rather cautious about exciting ideas. It listens with two ears, one hearing the meaning and the other listening for motives. Only the retreatant does the exercises suggested in *Spiritual Exercises,* while both retreatant and mentor should be engaged in praxis. While the practice side by itself runs the danger of becoming just a recipe for spiritual success, praxis links the exercises performed to the honest desires, questions, and concerns of the retreatant and mentor.

The difference between practice and praxis is relevant far beyond a retreat context. In general, practice refers to what individuals do or say or produce while praxis refers to the responsible, free choices that lie behind what they do or say or produce. Professionals find it a lot easier to talk about practice than about praxis (though not necessarily in these terms), but when the men and women they serve talk to each other, the topic is praxis. For example, doctors talk

about "my practice," with roughly the same meaning, while
their patients are concerned not only about the quality of
the practice they receive but about their doctors' intelligence, realism, and discretion—in other words, about their
praxis. The same goes for lawyers, teachers, and other
professionals. Certainly the people who hire them expect to
pay for a modicum of skill and information, but at the first
hint of poor judgment, they suspect that the services they
are receiving are not worth the money.

   With regard to the experience of retreat in particular,
practice, on the one hand, deals with the "spiritual exercises" a retreatant makes. The term also refers to the theological and psychological knowledge and to the manners
and style of both a retreatant and a mentor. Praxis, on the
other hand, refers to the wits to use the spiritual exercises
intelligently and to apply theological and psychological
knowledge when and where appropriate. It includes an
awareness of one's manners and a readiness to modify them
if it will help a conversation reach the depths of the mystery
of God and of life. Most important, praxis refers to that
ultimate art of religious discretion, the "discernment of
spirits."

## 2. DISCERNMENT OF SPIRITS

   Before talking about what discernment of spirits is, I
must say something about what it is not. It is not "discerning the will of God"—a confusing phrase that has crept into
religious parlance and, unfortunately, into the ways people
have been told to make good decisions. I have no idea where
the expression originated; it is certainly not in the writings
of Ignatius Loyola, who is generally credited with perfecting
the art of discernment. "Discern God's will" evokes an image
of some subtle method of discovering some information
about what God wants of me, followed, presumably, by my
carrying it out. It avoids the terrifying burden of freedom in
making a fully responsible decision in spite of uncertain-

ties—the kind of burden that weighed upon Jesus in Gethsemane. In the classic texts of Ignatius on making a major decision about one's state in life, he never uses the words *discern, know, find,* or *discover* in connection with God's will. He talks exclusively of *deliberating, weighing, choosing,* and *deciding.*[1]

What the expression *discernment of spirits* does refer to is the habit of noticing what is going on in one's psyche. The art of discernment, as Ignatius promoted it, dealt with "feeling and recognising in some manner the various motions that are excited in the soul,—the good that they may be taken up; the evil, that they may be rejected."[2] So the "spirits" in his "discernment of spirits" simply means the desires, the aversions, the proposals or the realizations that we experience. Usually we experience these inner events while we are focusing on something else—reading a book, reflecting on some practical matter, listening to someone talk, although there are times when these movements seize us without any apparent antecedents.

Ignatius wrote about these inner events primarily to help people understand the typical patterns of compulsion and grace in their lives so that they are not unwitting victims of their own biases. As it happens, people who have become familiar with how their pride and their love tend to work do not need "rules" for discernment when they face a major decision; they already know how to tell when their deliberation is reliable. But for people who have been oblivious to their inner experience and who now face a major decision, rules for discernment are usually too little too late.

In any case, while the attempt to "discern God's will" belongs to some rather dubious practice, "discernment of spirits," or "growing familiar with inner movements," clearly belongs to praxis. It is not psychological curiosity that impels us to want to grow in our ability to recognize what goes on in our psyches. We want to test whether our desires to do something concrete are consonant with our love for God. We perform that test by noticing whether there is an affective resonance between some actual good we hope to do and our life history of experiences of loving God, hoping in God, and loving our neighbor.

Since this discernment tests for an affective resonance between our present inner experience and our memories of past experiences of faith, hope, and charity, our ability to discern the spirits grows in proportion to our growth in several other areas.

Our ability to recognize trustworthy feelings and thoughts certainly grows in proportion to our prayer life, since that is where we allow our faith and hope in God to flood our consciousness. In prayer we become familiar with the experiences of noticing God's hand around us. We grow accustomed to depending on God for sticking with us in rough times, rather than spending our imagination on schemes of our own that promise more control over life than life can allow. By getting used to conversation with God year after year, we can more easily check to see if new ideas or projects do violence to these experiences of faith and hope. A surprising proportion of well-meaning men and women make their decisions sheerly on the objective worth of some proposal, ignoring completely the subjective call from God, a call that can be heard only by those who have learned the sound of God's voice. You can tell them by the anxieties that accompany their good works.

Discernment skills also grow in proportion to how passionately and genuinely we have cared for others. Pious souls who ignore the messy humanity around them typically make bad decisions about "doing good." They have not really identified with the poor in spirit, not really found in others an echo of their own profound poverty of spirit. It is men and women not of insular holiness but of solidarity with the suffering who have the knack for seeing divine possibilities in everything human.

Finally, our ability to recognize spiritual events grows in proportion to our ability to notice and remember inner experiences. This is by far the most neglected area in the art of discernment. To notice and remember inner events requires examinations of consciousness throughout the day, in which we recall not so much what we have done but what occurred to us, what movements stirred in our minds and hearts, and what possible relevance they may have to our daily lives.

The reason for this neglect, may I say, is that few people are trained to understand what the different events are that can occur in their consciousness. While many people can distinguish different feelings, few distinguish the differences between getting an insight and validating it or between making a judgment of fact and forming a judgment of value. Even women and men of the most sound judgment are seldom able to say by what standard or criterion they have been able to say, "I'm pretty sure."

Praxis, therefore, will mean learning firsthand about our experiences of seeing divine values around us, of depending radically on God, and of full-blooded caring for anyone along our road. But praxis also has the more intellectual task of deliberately paying attention to those experiences, naming them accurately, thinking about them, and remembering them. This gives a retreat mentor and a retreatant a common language to talk about the enormous range of spiritual experiences. When they both engage in praxis, the warrant for choosing a certain exercise is always human intelligence rather than some reputation of the mentor or some mystifying aura enshrouding certain spiritual techniques. The choice of a specific exercise is itself an exercise in taking responsibility rather than a riskless deferring to somebody else's opinion. The choice belongs primarily to the retreatant, with the mentor's help, not the other way around.

## 3. DISCERNMENT OF STORIES

Yet praxis is far more than discernment of spirits, at least as that art is usually understood. Discernment of spir-

its aims to bring to light whether or not the sources of our
feelings or thoughts are to be trusted. Our feelings and
thoughts are shaped by many values that we hold dear but
never question. What goes on in our heads and hearts is
largely prefabricated by a host of ideas about what we think
history and society and salvation are all about. And most of
these preconditioning ideas we inherited without ever noticing or challenging them. We might "discern" to our heart's
content but never question our theology of history, our ecclesiology, our ethics, our vested interests, even our own un-
acknowledged phobias and compulsions.

To make wise choices it is not enough to scrutinize the
quality of our desires. Since the great nineteenth-century
discoveries in economics, sociology, psychology, and historiography, we have inherited questions about many unnoticed factors that legitimize certain desires and outlaw
others. Karl Marx's atheism aside, at least he taught us how
socioeconomic institutions can produce a "false consciousness" in which we are rendered numb to various forms of
oppression. Likewise, Freud taught us to look beneath our
conscious desires for hidden motives and fears. Historical-
critical thinkers taught us that the stories we believe about
our communities—be they country or church or family—are
not unrevisable "truth." Rather, they are somebody's interpretation of experiences, with each interpretation sanc-
tioning one set of questions and desires while inhibiting
another set.

The art of discerning spirits certainly has helped many
men and women make wise choices, but it should now be
complemented by an educated suspicion about the very beliefs and values that as children we trusted wholeheartedly.
The cat is out of the bag. We can no longer "discern the
spirits" without facing the deeper question of just how far
our own tradition, our economic situation, and our own
psyches prevent certain "spirits" from ever moving in us in
the first place. In my own experience, people who rely on
discernment of spirits alone for their decisions seldom crit-

icize institutions or raise the possibility of their own neurosis.[3]

Let us call this complement to discernment of spirits a "discernment of stories." By that I mean a readiness to ask whether our desires may be overly restricted by a kind of myth—the myth, say, that the Bible contains the only truths necessary; or that life is ultimately tragic, or paradoxical, or threatening, or fertile, or complex, or simple, and so on. Each such myth, or story, limits the field of possible desires that we allow in consciousness. The Victorian Story inhibited sexual desires. The Faithful Churchgoer Story inhibits the spirit of prophecy in churches. The American Individualist Story inhibits individual hopes for shared living. Then there are the stories we tell ourselves about ourselves: "I am the Neglected Child." "I must be liked, no matter what." "I must succeed like Uncle Ben."

Our ability to distinguish between reliable and unreliable stories depends on how educated we are in alternative stories. We need to understand the various philosophies that have shaped Western consciousness. We should read the classic works of fiction that show how every King Lear has a Cordelia, a Regan, and a Goneril. Likewise, it helps to read good contemporary fiction and see films that focus on development of characters. We can learn about the vastly different ways in which people regard themselves and their lives. Retreat directors (spiritual mentors) who read only theology books, like the managers and engineers who read only technical literature, are usually dumbfounded at the behavior of strangers. They have heard no stories of how the dynamics of the spirit might possibly work out in someone else, something fiction does far better than psychology or biography.

Certainly each of us has heard some of the classic stories and seen the better films. But praxis listens to stories not so much for entertainment as for an answer to the recurring question, How do other people deal with their experiences of fear, anger, hope, poverty, love, faith, and so on?

Good writers do not tell us an answer; they portray a search for an answer, allowing us to compare the struggles of fictional characters with our own. This is why even disturbing stories like Flannery O'Connor's and disturbing films like Ingmar Bergman's are so valuable, even when the characters do not succeed in getting what they want. But, not to neglect Walt Disney and C. S. Lewis, praxis also asks the recurring question, What images of triumph in struggle touch me most deeply?

## 4. PRAXIS AND TRADITION

If praxis takes a careful attitude toward the stories that shape our lives, it can seem to verge on skepticism toward tradition. I have no doubt that this is true. Praxis is a hogback road with traditionalism sloping sharply off to right and skepticism dropping off to the left. We see people slipping off to one side or the other all the time. For example, some retreatants pound on heaven's door for clear answers from God while others ask just to make it through another rough day. I have the impression that the self-righteous legalists and the rabid liberals tend to grow or diminish together, as if by some hidden historical process they were deeply linked. A more likely explanation is that we are by nature more reactionary than responsible, more ready to meet a power we legitimately fear by mounting an equally strong opposing campaign rather than by wielding the subtler sword of wisdom.

But even many of those who do manage to keep a balance cannot explain how they do it; they exercise praxis without having thematized it as an intelligent alternative to both the gnosticism on the right and the agnosticism on the left. How does praxis go forward enriching a tradition without sliding off to either traditionalism or skepticism?

We should take a closer look at how praxis actually works in the formation and passing on of our traditions. The classical, canonical, and legal texts that shape a culture are themselves products of praxis. Our founding mothers and fathers were disturbed by some customs or needs of their time. They admitted to themselves that they did not understand what was bothering them. They attempted various solutions and, little by little, put together a vision or a plan that met concerns coming from their tradition, from their fellows, and from their own hearts. They took the responsibility of saying something in public a.. ` putting the heat on others to consider what they see. And if the reaction of their publics raised questions they hadn't thought of, they went back to the drawing board.

Although the public answers were designed to meet the needs of their own time, what made their texts venerable is that they survived the test of time. But what really is "the test of time" but the praxis of later generations doing exactly what the founders did? As the next generation faced new problems and formulated new questions, they discovered values lived out by a previous generation and formulated in some texts. This second generation reaffirmed those values and gave yet more muscle to the strength of the tradition. Praxis, therefore, not only was the activity that originated what was best in their traditions, it also remains the activity that best uses the tradition to meet each generation's problems.

I am not saying that the classics should tell us how to behave or think. Indeed, the reason some lovers of the classics stagger around like lost strangers on our planet today is that they are so enamored of the answers of the past that they shut their ears to the questions of today. It is better, it seems to me, to think of the classic works that anchor a healthy tradition not as having relevant answers but as having relevant questions. A university committee that reads about Plato's cave will likely wonder whether or not its curricula will help students get beyond fascination with the looks of things. A lawyer who reads *The Federalist* will begin to wonder whether his or her practice promotes government "by reflection and choice" instead of "by accident and force."

## 5. PRAXIS AND COMMUNITY

Praxis, then, means making one's own judgments about life, even when that judgment cuts across the traditional grain of a community. It understands fidelity not as blindly acting according to the formulations of inherited wisdom but as resolutely paying attention to what one's own spirit does with that wisdom. Where the heart differs from the heritage, praxis does not dig in its heels. Rather, it explores the difference with as open a mind as possible.

Here is where the praxis of retreat bumps up against the expectations of a community. After a retreat we return to everyday life hoping to act somehow differently in our home or workplace or with friends. But while we carry some notion of how we would like to act, we often have little notion of how others will react to us. Our private decision is exposed to the community's scrutiny and response. So the concrete exercise of praxis lies partly beyond our control as we meet unexpected reactions from the people around us.

Is this a reason for discouragement? It is certainly a fact of life that individual decisions are always tempered by communal responses. In other words, the spiritual life and the life of a community are inextricably linked, and that link is not always a healthy one. Some drop out of community as far as possible in order to get control of their spiritual lives. Others neglect a spiritual life in order to belong comfortably to a community. This is how life is. We cannot fully control the results of our decisions. But only the arrogant find this discouraging, since in their pride they think their decisions are always the best. The people who are intellectually and affectively free are grateful for the help a community can give in reaching as much objectivity as possible in discovering how best to act.

Let us look at what happens in a person who deals rather well with relating spirit to community in the concrete. Judy, a married woman with two teenage daughters, is thinking about going to law school. She hears the voices of her family. She can see what limits her financial situation puts on her. She even knows her own habitual way of dealing with career dreams. But she does not make any of these considerations ultimate. What is ultimate is her own intelligent, realistic, and wise assessment of these considerations at the moment. She is ready to scrutinize any of these voices and to take from them only what seems to her genuinely helpful. She knows that she can fool herself, but she also knows that she would rather not do so. If she does, her conscience will sour over unfinished business, and neglected feelings will burst out in inappropriate ways.

Praxis sets her at some distance from her own life-style, habits, commitments, and friends. So there is a solitude about praxis, not the affective loneliness that needs a warm hug, but an existential loneliness in which she alone decides on the company she wants to keep. She feels the ongoing risk that something inside of her might make her different from her neighbor and particularly from the familiar old self she has been.

Notice Judy's attitude toward the tension between her own spirit and the voice of her community. She relies on her intelligence, realism, and responsibility, but with a certain caution. She needs time to let further questions surface. She needs to incubate before she hatches any scheme. She has been wrong before and she may be wrong again. She relies on the traditions of her family, her church, and her culture not for answers on what to do but for questions that may not have occurred to her regarding her decision about law school.

It is in this interplay between her shared tradition and her personal deliberation that we understand exactly what makes a tradition rich and alive. She is keenly aware that her decision will have its disturbing effect on her role as wife and mother. Whatever she decides, their shared family values will take a relatively unpredictable turn. Moreover, she is aware of the inner effect this very deliberation will have on her overall ability to face tough questions. The more honest she is in this decision, the better able she becomes to face other decisions. It is this ongoing encounter between people of depth and their inherited traditions that makes the difference between a robust tradition and a meager one.

Suppose Judy now takes a few days of "retreat" to weigh all these considerations. Her heart is set not exactly on making "the best decision." That is, she does not imagine that an answer already lies somewhere for her to discover. She does not picture God as knowing but not telling. Nor is she concerned about the orderliness of the process. Her heart is set on the people who will be affected by her decision. In other words, the object of her praxis is the common good. It may be the good of unknown men and women in need of legal services, or the good of the family she knows well. In any case, that good includes herself as a vital member of some community. But it is love, not being right or being efficient, that gives praxis its purpose. Her retreat, her praxis, is for community, though probably not to preserve it in its present state.

## 6. TECHNIQUE

A praxis approach to spirituality is vastly different from another commonly held notion of how spirituality relates to action. In contrast to praxis, there is the more mechanical view that human actions should be guided by some technique.

There are many views on how some technique aims to substitute for the fuller resources of spirit. For one, there is the view that the body guides action. Here I am thinking of the misuse of such techniques as yoga and massage. Certainly our bodies condition and symbolize what is going on in our spirits. Certainly these techniques can dispose us for the more essential work of making wise choices in life. But many spiritual guides seem to have so little notion of the spiritual processes that constitute wisdom that they content themselves with directing the physical processes, as if our spirits were so opaque that we can only push and pull on human skin. By default they fail to deal intelligently and directly with bias, compulsion, and rationalization—the real enemies of the spiritual life of a community.

Another view that substitutes technique for wisdom states that analysis is enough to guide action. I am thinking here of systems such as the Myers-Briggs test and the Enneagram.[4] They have their place in analyzing past behavior, but they should never be used as guides to action—for example, "An INTJ should pray like this . . ." or "An Enneagram Six should act like a Nine." Action should be guided by free and responsible choice, not some analytical technique that substitutes for the heavier burden of taking responsibility.

Sad to say, even prayer is often used as a technique. We can faithfully beg God every day for what we need, dutifully fulfill our Sabbath obligations, "make" the retreat that everyone says we must make, and so on. But all this is only "doing" things. To the extent that these practices substitute for intelligent inquiry, for realistic assessments, and for brave, responsible decisions, they prevent us from tapping the spiritual resources God has given us.

I would especially like to point out here how love of technique will substitute not only for a retreatant's authentic responsibility but also for the mentor's own intelligence. This happens when, as a result of some analysis, we label another person with some category drawn from psychology or sociology. We name a man, say, "passive-aggressive" and thereby expect that any resistance he shows to our suggestions is nothing but stubbornness. We discount any resistance he may show toward something harmful. It being the nature of a label to end curiosity, we ignore his question whether there may be genuine danger in our suggestion.

We render ourselves functionally deaf to the retreatant's wisdom.

If we view a community as a large reservoir of intelligence, irrigating and replenishing the surrounding terrain with creative ideas, it becomes clear how categorizing other people diminishes the general fertility of the reservoir. The community's responses to some situations will be less effective simply because some members have used a label to dam the flow of certain kinds of insight. Thus, although it is commonplace to think of labeling others as "unfair," the real trouble is that it is stupid. It only diminishes the overall capacity of the community to meet its challenges.

There are a host of other techniques whose allure lies precisely in the promise of a shortcut around wise and intelligent deliberation. Technique hucksters are usually dogmatic about their systems. They have to be; dogmatism is the strongest defense against intelligent curiosity about exceptions to the rule and against the prudential judgments in applying laws. I would go so far as to say that anytime we hear echoes of dogmatism (particularly from ourselves), we can suspect that there lurk an overreliance on technique and a fear of the knotty reality of a situation.

## 7. LIBERATION PRAXIS

My notion of praxis differs not only from love of technique. It differs also from the definitions usually given by Marxists and liberation theologians. For them "praxis" is usually defined as something like "critical reflection on socioeconomic experience by the oppressed for the sake of liberation." The value of this definition is its suspicion of those social and economic institutions which ignore the experience of the marginalized. But the problem with such a definition is that it uses ambiguous physical metaphors rather than technical terms drawn from consciousness.

Take "oppressed" for example. Once the word enters conversation, the assumption is that the world is divided between oppressors and oppressed, and an adversarial view of life is taken for granted. Yet many social thinkers disagree that the basic way to view humanity is in terms of warring power groups. A more astute analysis discovers that the powerless usually interiorize the values of the powerful to such an extent that they believe they deserve their woeful lot. At the same time, the so-called powerful spend more and more intellectual energies protecting the system against change and less on intelligent responses to other social and economic crises. In the long run they lose the power to meet crises. Thus an "oppressive" situation is a self-sustaining system maintained by both the powerful and the powerless and in which both become its victims. Note that this kind of analysis examines value judgments and insights—events in consciousness—rather than drawing conclusions from mere images of some vicious oppressors pushing down on the hapless oppressed.

Likewise for "liberation." What on earth does that mean exactly? The word conjures up an image of escaping from some kind of imprisonment, but it does not reveal the nature of that imprisonment. Likewise, terms like *racism* or *sexism*, while they inflame our emotions, leave our understanding stagnant. Even if that imprisonment were spelled out in legal, economic, and social terms, there is still the massive task of creating an alternative. Does "liberation" envisage any positive social program? Without a clear social theory backing up the term, there is no way to derive strategic principles by which a people can be galvanized to achieve such a liberation.

In the pages to follow we will envision a society and a culture as products of insight, judgments, agreements, and the biases of consciousness that infect these processes. These are the processes of spirit that both spiritual mentors and retreatants need to understand—first in themselves and then insofar as these processes make or break the society they live in.

## 8. THE CIRCLE OF PRAXIS

I would like to group the many processes of praxis under four headings: (1) noticing the concrete situation, (2) meditating on its meaning, (3) contemplating its truth and worth, and (4) deliberating about the choice that is the purpose of the retreat. These will form the topics of chapters 5 through 8.

A retreat does not end with a choice, however. Once a fundamental choice is made, the processes of praxis reverse themselves, so that there comes a need to *contemplate* the full, divine reality of one's choice, to *meditate* on the theological and practical ramifications of the choice, and to *notice* people and events in the world around one in terms of the religious vision upon which the choice was made.

As you read, therefore, be aware that the processes of praxis form a kind of circle, as shown in the figure on p.31. The circle is not a recipe to follow. One may discover the need to jump from one part of the circle to another, either to anticipate problems or to correct oversights. The circle is meant to represent how the different processes intervene between choice and the concrete situation. I have not written a chapter on either choice or the concrete situation. I can only talk in general about what goes on in our minds and hearts as we engage our world responsibly.

Before beginning with the praxis of noticing, there are two topics that form the context of the rest—surrounding the circle, as it were. First is the topic of "God." As I have already intimated, we need to be continuously ready to learn more about God from experience. In chapter 3 I will speak of God in terms of our experiences of being related to the divine and as the primary relationship that we assess and reintegrate in a retreat.

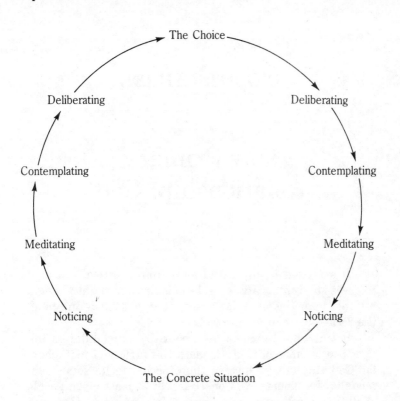

The other topic is "history." The circle of praxis makes little sense unless it is set against the background of a vision of history that sets human choice as the most crucial factor in its unfolding. Therefore, in chapter 4 I will speak of an "imaginal theology of history," by which I mean a symbolic (not theoretical) representation of what human history is all about.

# CHAPTER THREE

# Our Primary Relationship: God

If a retreat is any withdrawal from practical concerns to assess and integrate our relationships, we ought to begin by looking at the one relationship that gives meaning to all the rest—our relationship to God.

Recall what I said earlier about the many different images people have of God. Beneath the variety of metaphors for God throughout history there seems to lie some commonality in experience. Consequently, at least when people of different religions talk about "God" together, they will understand each other much better if they connect their beliefs to the underlying historical experiences of the founders. It does little good simply to cite authorities to people who do not acknowledge them as authorities.

This kind of conversation ought to happen not only between people of different cultures but even within each person as he or she grows up. Our own metaphors for God will change as our emotional and intellectual developments require corresponding developments of our faith. To approach the real God afresh, we need to return to our experience again and again, discovering new questions and further answers that arise out of that experience. Those new questions, after all, deal partly with whether or not the very authorities that provided answers to our earlier questions experienced our present dilemmas.

Far from repudiating traditional doctrines of God, this approach enlivens them. What tradition has taught about God is usually expressed in lean propositions that conceal their historical birthplace. The propositions are true enough, but they will not have any real significance for latter-day believers unless they can be related to personal experiences—experiences one hopes are very much like the engendering experiences from which the doctrines were first developed. For example, the doctrine that we should forgive the offenses of others will mean nothing to a person who has never felt desperate for forgiveness from others. Our assent to the propositional statements becomes a real rather than mere notional assent only when the statements make sense of our experience. A retreat is a splendid time to realize the meaning of these saving doctrines for our own lives.

We also saw that there are two sources of our knowledge of God. One is what we have heard from other people, and the other is what we have learned firsthand within our own hearts. And in each of these sources, long before we learned anything new about God's relation to us, there burned an experience and a question. It will help us learn the praxis of retreat if we understand clearly which experiences usually raise the question of God in our lives.

## 1. THE DOUBLE QUESTION OF GOD

Have you ever in your life given orders to the morning or sent the dawn to its post?

Has the rain a father?
Who begets the dewdrops?

What womb brings forth the ice and gives birth to the frost of heaven when the waters grow hard as stone?

Can you fasten the harness of the Pleiades or untie the belt of Orion?

Will lightning flashes come at your command and answer,
"Here we are"?

Do you know how mountain goats give birth, or have you ever
watched the hinds in labor?

(Jb 38:12, 28–29, 31, 35; 39:1)

There can be little doubt, even among atheists, that the
question about God will always be with us.[1] Anytime we
look at creation and allow ourselves to realize that *it did
not have to be,* we cannot help but wonder why the earth,
the heavens, and ourselves happen to be and whence we
came.

However, the more persistent and universal question
about God throughout history has not been the one discussed in schools and celebrated in religious poetry and art.
We hear it rather cried out in hospitals and on battlefields:
*Why do the innocent suffer?* What have we done to deserve
the horrors of war, political oppression, racial and sexual
apartheid, betrayal by friends, mental breakdowns, and
physical diseases? Even where the question is not put into
words, the pain in every silent suffering is multiplied by the
unanswered question *why.* It is far more important to hear
that question—to *feel* that question—than to dote on abstract discussions about whether a God exists.

Particularly for women and men who, having escaped
suffering for a time, enjoy the comforts of peace and the
pride of achievements, it is important not to forget that God
has never answered our Why? question. To experience in
ourselves the question about God we must remember the
wounded and the dead. There is a tendency in all of us,
when we hear stories of great pain and tragedy, to look for
someone to blame or, if not blame, at least to draw some
lesson from the past. This is salutary, of course; the perpe-
trators of evil should be stopped and the lessons of history
should be learned. But these reactions should not draw us
too far from the stunning moment in which we could
scarcely believe the story. To allow the truth of incompre-

hensible violence and death to be told and remembered entails suffering a question we cannot answer. It provokes us to cry out to the heavens for a justification. We not only realize with our minds, we feel in our hearts how we stand in solidarity with the human race, even with those who bury the question in the soil of forgetfulness.

Elie Wiesel's *Night,* about the atrocities against German Jews, is a story to remember, to contemplate without asking too quickly, Who's to blame? and What's the moral of this story? It is a story to stand vigil with. Simply reading the narrative is an exercise in not turning our heads away but becoming the witness, even an accuser of God, simply by remembering. Wiesel's story can teach us how to read the Passion narratives in the Gospels, which have become distorted by moral lessons and paeans to suffering. Jesus, who is the teacher of the highest moral standards in the early chapters of the Gospels, stands mute and suffers, asking only, "Why, Father, have you forsaken me?" And God is silent. Just as Wiesel's story can show us how to read the Passion, the Passion, in turn, should teach us how to read the signs of our own times.

Good art can help us experience the unformulatable question of God's relationship to us as we witness human misery. Picasso's *Guernica,* portraying the savage bombing of a small Spanish village, cries a universal petition. Van Gogh's *Potato Eaters* gather to enjoy, with pitiable dignity, the humble fruits of the earth. It is all about rueful human effort, and the implicit question, How long, O Lord?

The other universal source of questions about God is our own souls. We are frustrated yet hopeful. Nothing satisfies us, yet something constantly drives us toward getting satisfaction. No matter how horrible the stories of human self-destruction and misery, we wake up one morning and discover the courage to make the best of things.

Just as we ought to contemplate the cry of the poor, so we ought to contemplate this pull we experience upon our souls. Some inner current quietly carries us toward creating something of infectious natural beauty, something of dignity and elegance.[2] This too is a species of suffering. We are passive regarding its origin and direction. And when we let it draw us along, we become a kind of victim of a love we feel for another person, for a home, for the world.

Some days we feel it, and some days we do not. Yet most days we act under the power of that dark love. Just as recalling human suffering leaves us with the unanswered question *Why,* so this inner passion asks *who.* Who is this that draws us? How can we love someone we cannot see? Who is this that can give us the very love with which we love? For some the answer is "nobody"; but they give no more convincing evidence for their answer than those who answer "God."

Loving one's neighbor becomes a catharsis for this love that cannot touch or see its beloved. There is a joy and a satisfaction in centering our affections on this friend, this family, this community, the people of this land. We know it is right because everything else in our souls springs to life and works harmoniously. We easily forget that the *who* question remains unanswered unless we return to prayer, or to philosophical reflection, to contemplate the great mystery that is our own spirits turning toward the light without asking our permission.

Good music can help direct our attention to this inner pull. The tensions and development of musical themes echo not so much mystery's visible forms, which art does so well, as our visceral responses to that mystery. Each instrument represents a different voice within us searching for its own satisfactions while trying to accommodate, overcome, submit to, or harmonize with other voices making their own search. The best compositions resonate with voices inside us that we never noticed before, and so we return to the music again and again to befriend those inner voices, to learn how they speak in the strings, the woodwinds, and the brass sections of our psyches.

At first we do not notice that the question of God is double. This is because the inner question and the outer question always occur together. To see suffering is to suffer. To really hear about anything human is to become more human. To remember someone laughing is to laugh again. Both art and music, with their different emphases, carry external, sensible forms to internal feelings and imagination. In both the seen and the seeing, the heard and the hearing, we sense the mystery of something more, always more. This is a direct experience of our relationship to God, which is an experience of being drawn, pulled, invited. Plato described it as being dragged out of a cave where fascination with mere shadows prevails and into the sunlight of the real. Matthew described it as being invited by an intinerant preacher to follow him. Dag Hammarskjöld described it as having said "Yes" to a question he could not formulate.

For the sake of authentic praxis in spirituality, it is essential to recognize, name, cherish, and grow increasingly familiar with the experience of this double mystery in life. Religious experience is not something to be sought after, as if we seldom felt it. It is something we always feel but need to notice and familiarize ourselves with. A retreat is not a time to wait for God to make a move; it is a time to notice the moves God is making.

## 2. GOD'S DOUBLE RESPONSE

To these questions of *why* and *who* God has already responded, although not with an explanation or a lucid piece of information; that is, God has not answered the question in the form expected by our posing it. It is a "response" much more engaging than any verbal or visual response ever could be. Likewise, it is a double response to our double experience and double question. Let us name this strange response an *outer Word* and an *inner Word*.[3]

The outer Word speaks through the very universe whose marvels raised the question in the first place. It is a response that came before the question. The discovery of that love may be compared to a child of undemonstrative parents discovering as a teenager the great sacrifices they made without demanding a return. Prior to that discovery the home was simply "there," the parents were simply "there"—so much so that their sleepless nights of worry and their hard work to make ends meet went unnoticed and, as part of love's gift, discounted.

Once a community acknowledges the universe as a Word of God's love, the community itself becomes part of that Word. It is, after all, part of the universe. But it plays a part far more significant than the wonders of nature. History itself becomes a Word of God in this believing community as it takes God's attitude toward the marginalized, spells out its beliefs in divine mystery, and preaches love and reconciliation to others. In other words, the outer Word of God includes the stories, laws, and covenants, the paintings, sculpture, and music, and especially the flesh-and-blood persons that make a religion alive.

Unfortunately, religions have earned bad reputations. It is easy to think of world religions as paths toward God, paths unfortunately overgrown and entangled with the cares of the world. We find it difficult to think of the very phenomenon of religion as God's path to us, a Word of truth and beauty.

For this reason we make a distinction between the official religion, with all its buildings, rules, liturgies, and traditions, and the actual men and women who love the world with God's love. There is no membership list for this community; it is leaven in the dough. Yet their own truth and beauty are not far below the surface. We can be touched by people who struggle to be faithful to God. We learn about God from our parents, usually, taking them as a Word of God in this sense. The term *apostolic,* considered to be a distinguishing mark of a true Christian church, does not mean "missionary," as its Greek root might suggest. It means that our faith believes in the historical experience of the *apostles,* of the human beings who first experienced something new in history, many of whom seem to have returned to a hidden life after the Resurrection.

Belief in one's church is belief not in a human tower that can reach up to God but in a divine descent into human history. History itself, then, carries a Word from God that speaks to human suffering through the very love and care of one person for another and through any human teachings about human solidarity.

In the historical Jesus of Nazareth, Christians believe that God has gone far beyond mere messages, teachings, and symbols. After giving many "words" to the world, again and again, in thousands of different ways, God has finally "given his word" in the sense of having made an irrevocable commitment to living with us. God has come in person. Jesus is the Word of God par excellence. He comes not to abrogate all other aspects of the outer Word but to give them meaning through his life and death. He taught not only that to see him was to see the Father but that to give a cup of water to any human being was to give a cup of water to him. By his teaching and his example he settled an ambiguity about how we should respond to this pull we experience that draws us into divine mystery. Our response to God's love for us is not to "return" that love to God; it is to give that love to neighbor. "Since God has loved us so much, we too should love one another" (1 Jn 4:11).

So God has not answered our *why* question with an explanation. Rather, God has stood by our side and asked the question with us. In Jesus, God has witnessed the mystery of evil in his own personal agony, without blaming or moralizing. Jesus is both our primeval human cry (what sufferer is more innocent?) and God's perfect Word in response. In witnessing the deed of Jesus we have come to understand that suffering and death, no matter how painful, are not the worst things that can happen to a person. The worst thing is not what can harm the body but what casts the soul into hell. It is hatred of the light, revulsion over truth, resistance to what is good, and rejection of beauty that constitute what ought to be the true object of our horror. These certainly result in the destruction of life in others, but the first death is within the person sinning against his or her own better spirit.

The outer Word of God is not restricted to the person of Jesus. By "person," after all, we normally mean someone *connected* to others at a fixed point in *history,* someone whose being is limited by parents, locale, and body. What the first disciples saw and believed in was not simply the individual Jesus, considered in abstraction from his Jewish concerns, his motley group of friends, and his sincere compassion for this blind man and that arthritic woman. When they saw what Jesus did and heard what he said, their first question was about what *God* was up to in history. Is this the Messiah whom God promised to send? Has the long-awaited Day of the Lord finally arrived? Jesus himself kept deflecting questions about himself and pushing the question of whether the Reign of God was near or not.

The first disciples welcomed Jesus as the Word and work of God. They realized that God's Word in Jesus was meant to be a continuing Word preached and lived out by Christians. They themselves were to "make up all that has still to be undergone by Christ" (Col 1:24). They themselves "will perform the same works, even greater works" as Jesus (Jn 14:12). They become transformed from people who question God about injustice to people who are God's response to those who suffer.

It could be no other way. If God's response is to come in the person of one who joins the sufferers, this Word must continue as long as history keeps flowing forward; that is, the Christian vocation is not merely to teach but to join, to accompany, to engage the human. Such is the nature of God's response.

This Christian teaching does not deny that God continues to speak an outer Word to other religions or even to people of no religion. There is an "anonymous Christ" wherever someone lovingly responds to the sufferings of another. Regardless of what he or she thinks is going on, a powerful Word of love is spoken.

Likewise, this teaching does not leave creation itself out of the picture. Most people, in fact, find it rather easy to believe that God speaks in creation; the difficulty is believing whether God also speaks in *history*. Just think of how much easier it is to marvel at a starry night than at the craggy face of a beggar. But once we believe the good news that in Jesus, God has become irrevocably human—to the point of being irrevocably hooked up with historical peoples—the entire meaning of the cosmos, from unseen galaxies to unseeable subatomic particles, becomes focused on the Word in history. Then we have to take a new look at the whole of creation. Nature is not a Word of God separate from the Word in history. Somehow the significance of the universe is, or will be, connected to the historical meaning of Christ Jesus. This is the vision of the hymn in Colossians: "in him were created all things in heaven and on earth" (1:15–20).

Corresponding to this outer Word of God in history and the cosmos is an inner Word of God in our hearts. Again, this is not an inner message or doctrine from which we draw conclusions. Nor is it a clear answer to our question *Who*. Yet it is truly a "response" from God. The response has the character of an inner experience of *desire*. Besides the question arising from the experience of an inner pull, we also experience a commitment, a devotion, a kind of falling in love with an inner source that makes new persons of us. When we commit ourselves to trusting this inner pull toward what is good and true, we begin to notice an unexpected discretion about practical affairs and a surprising patience with the shortcomings of others. Like the falling in love that leads to marriage, when we accept this inner pull, when we stop resenting its failure to give us that elusive control and security we wish we had, the world takes on a beauty for us that we had not noticed before.

We "hear" God's response when we yield to the pull and let it take control of our lives. Like the outer Word that shares our history, the inner Word joins our love. As the

outer Word is a person-in-relation-in-history, the inner Word
is a love that builds personal relationships in history. It is
God's intimate gift of the very power and act of love—a love
beyond what we could expect of ourselves. We begin to value
the world with God's own eyes and to love the world with
God's own love.

This love, in fact, is experienced as prior to the outer
Word. We would not recognize God in the cosmos, in the
teachings and deeds of religions, and in Christ Jesus if we
were not already somehow in love with absolute truth and
goodness. People recognize the divine Word in Jesus Christ
because they are already moved by God's own Spirit. All
throughout the New Testament the role of the "Holy Spirit"
is not to give new messages but to give an eye to recognize
which of the known messages come from God. The meaning
of the doctrine that God offers salvation to all is equivalent
to the doctrine that God's love is in the heart of everyone,
capable of discovering God's Word in history, and capable of
selling everything for this pearl of great price.

I have described our experience of God as, first, the experience of a double question and, second, the experience of
a double response. This is indeed how we experience it. Yet
once we accept God's response to our questions, we realize
that we have not initiated the conversation at all. In our
awareness, our questions were first; but in *reality,* God's
Words of love were first. The truth is that God had always
been addressing us—through history and through our
hearts—and that the needed response is to come from us.

It is extremely important, however, particularly for
spiritual directors or teachers, not to begin at the end. We
very frequently hear from preachers how much God loves
us, as if that knowledge will solve all our problems. It is
certainly true that God loves us first, but people on the
search do not need to hear this. They need to honor the
search itself, to feel the painful question, to consider the possibility that God is responding to them through the church
and within their own hearts. Lead them to recognize how
much they love God: the search itself is the evidence. Then

the questions can be posed, Who gave you this love? Why was this love given to you? Does not the source of this love *love* you? In other words, lead them up to the insight, but let them discover in their personal experience of the search itself the overwhelming evidence of God loving them by a double self-donation.

Likewise for the outer Word of God-with-us. Telling people that Jesus Christ is God among us, that he heals all our ills, and that we should cast all our cares upon him can be mere rhetoric to people who are suffering. Jesus can sound like some kind of spiritual opium that will lift a person out of history somehow to give him or her some heavenly solace. This is heresy. Much better to begin with the humanity of Jesus, with the Gospel narratives of a real historical person going about doing good, and the horror of his persecution and death. Become a witness to what happened to this great-hearted man. Then listen to the proclamation that God has given this Jesus life, raised him up, giving him the name above all names. It is a proclamation. It is news. A person does not have to believe it; it cannot be proved. Yet for the person who takes it as true, the gift of Christ, as God's perfect Word and gift of the divine self to human history, begins to dawn.

Just as in the human fetus we see earlier evolutionary forms of the mature human body, so in being "born again" we begin with the earlier historical experiences of the human cry and the human Jesus. In the pedagogy of spirituality, then, there are two precepts for those on the search. First, it is usually better to begin with our love for God; God's love for us will be rediscovered as primary. Second, it is usually better to begin with Jesus the human; Jesus the divine will be rediscovered as primary.

## 3. SHARED LIFE WITH GOD

Our relationship to God, then, is double. God gives the divine self to us in a way no human person could. God "speaks" a person who comes in history, and God "wel-

comes" in us the very Word spoken. So far, I have not mentioned the Christian doctrine of the Trinity. The reason is
that we had to retrieve the spiritual experiences of those
who formulated that doctrine. But now we can see why we
believe that one God is somehow three. If the real God has
truly given the divine self to us, and that self-gift is a double
gift, the "speaking" and "welcoming" through which we experience God must be truly part of God. The one God truly
has a multiplicity, which theologians eventually named "two
processions." It is on account of God's natural "speaking"
and "welcoming" that God is three—One speaking, One spoken, and One welcoming.

Yet there is more about this double relationship God
has established with us. God shares the divine life with us
in a manner that expects us to be actively cooperating as
well as passively welcoming. The inner and outer Words of
God are not gifts merely for our delight and comfort. God
labors in us to make a better world. This is a wonderful
kind of shared work that God offers us. On the one hand,
God is not using us as mere instruments for the good of
others; God genuinely desires our own joy, our own happi-
ness, our own consolation. Misery is a sure sign of false
prophets—people miserable over all that they cannot accomplish for others while completely neglecting the joy God offers them. On the other hand, God does not want us simply
to hide the inner and outer Word under a basket; being
God's very self-gift, we should naturally overflow in love to
others. Compassion (which misery feigns) is a sure sign of
a true prophet.

How do the inner and outer Words overflow? The spirit
of God within always seeks what is good, what is true, what
makes sense. God seeks it in the concrete, seeks it every
day. The Word of God in history addresses us through the
example of others, through religious traditions, through art
and song and dance, calling us to get beyond the selves that
we are.

When we respond to God's inner and outer address to
us, the spirit rejoices in us over every insight, every realiza-

tion, every recognition of anything good. We then speak a word. We offer our insight to a situation. We stand up for the truth. We let our feelings show in what we find valuable and beautiful, as well as in what we find repulsive and ugly.

These divinely impelled human acts change our concrete situation, usually for the better. This is God at work in us redeeming the world where we stand. We have become part of the outer Word of God every time we contribute something meaningful or valuable to life.

This is a simple vision, really. Christians have always believed that religion was somehow good for the world, but they have not always understood how. Certain otherworldly spiritualities preached a love of God that was a love *for* God that dispensed people from obligations to love their neighbor. Then there have been the doctrinaire spiritualities—of women and men who believed that the teachings of their church, precisely as they formulated them, were the "message" God wanted them to parrot, without any intelligent and sensitive consideration for the situation of their audience and still less willingness to join the marginalized in their cry for redemption. Still others have embraced a spirituality of Christian moralism—reasoning that since God has given us so much, we have certain obligations to fulfill to pay for the gift. This vision ignores altogether the intimate gift of self that God gives us without condition.

The doctrines on God that we have been working toward here are not statements about nature and persons. Rather, they are statements about actions and relationships. Those "retreating" to reassess some relationships in their lives will do well to consider these primary relationships to God. Given all we have said so far, it may be helpful to summarize some of these basic truths.

- God speaks to us both in the cosmos of nature and in the vicissitudes of history.

- God speaks to us within our own hearts whenever we are inclined toward the beautiful, the true, the good.

- The historical Jesus of Nazareth, including all his friendships, memories, teachings, and effect on subsequent history, is God's outer Word to us.

- God makes us part of that outer Word whenever we act on the values that Jesus lived and taught.

- We act on these values only under the power of a gift of love, which is God's own spirit, dwelling in our hearts.

- Some of the values that Jesus revealed are turn the other cheek; walk the second mile; beware not those who can kill the body but those who kill the soul; love your neighbor as yourself; the poor in spirit are happy; be compassionate as your heavenly Father is compassionate; trust in God.

- Rejoice. The Kingdom of God is yours.

## 4. THE BROKEN RELATIONSHIP

We can break off our relationship to God in many ways. We lie, we rob, we kill. Yet these deeds do not constitute the essence of our sin; any high school sophomore can make a case for these deeds' legitimacy in certain circumstances. As we did with the doctrines about God, we need to pull back from what we have been taught and start again from our experience. There we will see clearly the true essence of a broken relationship with God.

We saw that God relates to us in the most intimate way imaginable: by the donation of the divine, double Word. These are God's gift of the divine self. Gifts of love. Permanent gifts. Christ will never leave his humanity, and every human person experiences the draw of God's own spirit within.

Our first response, it seems to me, ought to be a loving appreciation, an abiding gratitude. That means noticing the inner and outer Word every day. It means realizing for oneself that God is freely and actively donating the divine self to us in our history and in our hearts. It means humbly and happily accepting our role in becoming the continuation of God's outer Word for others. It means remembering these deeds of the Lord and praising God in thankfulness.

The first fissures in this relationship show when we forget what this world and we really are. We have the power to break God's relationship with us simply by not remembering. We take things "for granted" without noticing that Someone grants them. Once we forget that the land and sea, the natural resources, even time itself are gifts, we then think of them in terms of *property*. Greed sets in. We become panic-stricken when we lose anything. Even people become property to us as we try to enforce a control over our employees or spouses that we would never allow over ourselves.

Then a different spirit takes over our consciousness. We no longer entertain all questions. We allow only those questions that show promise for our benefit. We refuse to take a hard look at first one truth, usually about what is happening to us, then another and another until truth itself becomes merely instrumental to what we think is our own welfare. We stop appreciating the good around us; we stop dreaming of the good for anyone else. Soon we cannot tell the difference between what is truly good and what is merely comfortable for ourselves.

It is within this distorted consciousness that the deeds of sin arise—lying, thievery, killing. Then the inner distortion becomes a social and a historical distortion. Even if no one went so far as to rob or kill, there is still the sin of muzzling the spirit of inquiry, sincere wonder, and goodhearted hope. From the point of view of history, we become a dead spot where no life can be expected. An aggregate of dead spots—that is, a group of people who have forgotten God's gifts—becomes increasingly chaotic as outrageous solutions are applied to outrageous problems. The Dominion of God has definitely receded.

So there are two fundamental kinds of spirit in human consciousness. One kind loves the light, the other hates it. One trusts that the full truth is better than any partial truth; the other fears that some truth will kill. One delights in the mind's free play; the other whips the mind into serving only the person in whose head it resides.

The practice of "discernment of spirits" and the practice of "discernment of stories" aim to make an issue of our split consciousness, catching sin at its innocent-looking root. One root is consciously experienced. It is a matter of our spirits. We can notice the quality and the tone of our ideas and emotions. The other root is relatively unconscious. It is a matter of stories that we believe without remembering exactly where we heard them. They arise either from repressed psychological material, making us somewhat neurotic, or from a social oppression that assigns us a fixed role in life.

But we have God's pledge to dwell in us as a Spirit stronger than any spirit. And we have God's pledge to dwell in our history as a Word with the power to break the ideologies and myths that tell us we are less than we truly are.

Again, those facing major decisions in life need to be aware of their real sinfulness. Many people come to a retreat with a shamefaced and admirable readiness to admit wrongdoing. But that is not enough. There is yet a more shameful forgetfulness of God's love to acknowledge. While God's love has surrounded them in history and flowed within them in their hearts, they have tried to live life— often a "religious" life—on their own. I do not think it is false humility for the more famous saints to think of themselves as the greatest sinners. Their sin truly is enormous. After realizing the intensity of God's love for humankind and for themselves, they blithely abandoned the truth and lived again in a self-centered dream. They know that there is less excuse for this than for most robberies, lies, and murders.

As inner disobedience to the divine pull shows up in greed and hatred, people cease trusting one another. A family is no longer bound together by a common gratefulness to God. A culture withdraws from a common wonder in and welcome of the universe. Nations take their stand on maintaining ownership of property, first by appeals to reason and, when fear outreaches reason, by appeals to that fear through threats of brute force and a political policy of balance of powers.

In this fashion, as the inner Word is stifled, the outer Word of God becomes barely distinguishable from mere babble in our communities. Greed and hatred become rationalized, institutionalized, legitimated, protected, and energetically taught to the young. It is in this kind of historical situation that most lying, robbing, and killing occur. We would like to pin the guilt on the perpetrator, but that culpability is usually connected to a deeper culpability of an entire community that has made inner disobedience a virtue.

## 5. THE SYMBOL "KINGDOM OF GOD"

Christians have referred to God's response to sin as the "Kingdom of God" or, in Matthew, the "Kingdom of heaven." As we might expect, the descriptive power of the language works well in homilies but poorly in theological understanding. Still, if our spiritual praxis is to work regularly with concrete experience, we will need the power of symbols to focus the clarity of understanding. I would like, therefore, to examine the merits of keeping the terminology of the Kingdom as a symbolic representation of a reality that concerns us all.

To begin with, I believe that "Kingdom" would be a much better symbol for our highest aspirations than the currently popular notion of "community." Many proponents of both liberation theology and conservative neo-orthodoxy perceive community as a product of goodwill and the solution to the world's problems. But our communities are selfish by nature. We may provide a loving atmosphere that converts selfish individuals to group concern, but the very sentiments and imaginations we ply to strengthen our in-

tramural bonds are also used to prevent accommodating our
resources to the needs of some other community.

Moreover, even where certain individuals do form a
community that has concerns wider than itself, this does
not reach the core of the problem of evil. The problem of evil
is not essentially that people are at odds with each other. It
is that people are at odds with themselves. When the eventual manifestation of inner hatred of the light breaks down
social bonds, we discover that a community is destroyed.
"Community" is not a solution itself. Community is rather
the *result* of the more radical solution provided by God's
double Word.

As an ideal to be reached, the "Kingdom" goes far beyond "community." From its beginnings in Scripture it has
represented the desire and the work of God, while "community" easily neglects mention of God, often degenerating
into nothing more than the desire and work of its members.
As a dynamic, historical project of a Someone, the Kingdom
connotes a process on the move. It develops. It is neither
nostalgic nor static, as communities tend to be. In the Kingdom we struggle, but always with hope. Its direction is not
set by ourselves alone but by a divine King who works, to
borrow a metaphor from Irenaeus, with one hand in our
history and the other in our hearts.

So I do not favor representing our highest aspirations
with the ideal of community because the term conveys neither the reality of the sin endemic to any community nor the
God whose inner and outer Words alone can heal the divi-
sions that badger every community.

Still, I see several difficulties with the term *Kingdom*.
(1) The historical use of the term has been highly ambiguous since the first century. (2) It does not offer a metaphor
people are familiar with today. (3) It connotes a male in
charge. (4) Even in Scripture the term does not represent,
by itself, the full, redemptive work of God. Let us look at
each of these difficulties more closely.

First, "Kingdom" has received ambiguous meanings in history. "The Kingdom" is essentially a New Testament term, although the notion of God as King over Israel certainly runs through the entire Old Testament.[4] The Kingdom Jesus proclaimed was something about to happen to a historical community. His listeners heard in his preaching a fulfillment of a Jewish apocalyptic hope for a new historical epoch for Israel. It relied on a common periodization of history into six ages: Adam-Abraham, Abraham-Moses, Moses-David, David-Exile, Exile-Messiah, Messiah-Final Age. This Kingdom is not an individual, spiritual reality but rather a communal, historical one. The "justice, peace, and joy" (Rom 14:17) of the Kingdom are not private dispositions; they are justice between peoples, peace rather than war, and a communal joy over this work of God.

Soon, however, various theologians diverted this apocalyptic-eschatological vision of the Kingdom into three distinctive streams. In a spiritual / mystical stream, championed by Origen, the Kingdom was focused on the individual's soul and on the afterlife. In a political stream, Constantine's ideologue, Eusebius of Caesarea, identified the Kingdom with a specific historical monarchy. And finally, reacting to Eusebius' civic Kingdom, Augustine created an ecclesial stream that regarded the Kingdom, the "City of God," as present in the church but ultimately and essentially in the afterlife.

While the views of Origen and Augustine contain profound truths, neither view holds that redemption can be understood as part of historical process itself. The political stream does take history more seriously, but only by ignoring any transcendent factors beyond political institutions. Even the original apocalyptic-eschatological vision, which looked to history for God's work on our behalf and included a hope in an afterlife, did not root the good news in a philosophical context equal in scope to the philosophical contexts of the various divergent developments.

A second difficulty with the term *Kingdom* is that it is an unfamiliar metaphor. Most people today have no experience of a king, still less of a kingdom. In particular, we do not have the experiences of loyalty, love, and service regarding a king that many monarchical cultures had.

Granted, a major exception to this is the genuine love that members of religious orders feel for their superiors general or that many Catholics feel for the pope. But these "monarchs" do not talk about "their" kingdoms; they speak only of the Kingdom of God, which leaves us without an analogy against which we can test what our relationship to that Kingdom might be.

A third difficulty is that Kingdom and its cognates in many languages connote a male in charge—a king. Here we must look at the feminist critique of Christian consciousness. We are only recently discovering the damage to human hopes that sheerly male images of God and God's redemption have done to our psyches. It is difficult for women to believe that they are made in God's image and likeness, and that their share in the sufferings of the body of Christ are just as vital as any man's. Correspondingly, it is difficult for men to believe that they are not the only ones expected to deal with the world's problems and therefore that they are not the only ones truly guilty of the world's ills. It is difficult for both sexes to identify equally with the Motherhood of Mary, understood as a person made worthy to bear the eternal Word of God to the world. Finally, it is difficult enough to explore the issues of legitimate authority in our churches without being completely distracted by the fact that it is chiefly men who have held jurisdiction. Why add to the burden by canonizing "Kingdom" to represent our fondest hopes?

My last critique is that Kingdom by itself is insufficient to represent our hopes. I am not saying we should outlaw the term altogether. Rather, like every metaphor for God, it should stand among others, each of which represents a truth none of the others do. The reality to which Jesus was pointing by his expression "Kingdom of God" is indeed mysterious. He had to use parable after parable to reveal all its aspects. Paul seems to use the term to refer to an impending afterlife, while talking about "the mystery hidden for ages" to refer to God's entrance into history and plan to extend salvation to the entire historical community. If, with Aquinas, we say that we can speak of God only by analogies, is not the same true of the Kingdom of God, which is a divinization not merely of individuals but of the sociohistorical human race as a unity extending beyond time into God's eternity?

The only conclusion I can come to in light of these difficulties is to follow the example of New Testament writers. They used a plurality of titles for Jesus simply because no one term could adequately represent the mystery of his person. It is in the very plurality of titles converging on Jesus, each partly illuminating and partly obfuscating, that the reader senses in him the "beyond" that Christians eventually identified, in a philosophical mode, as equality with God.

Consequently, I propose a constantly shifting approach to the mystery of the community-in-history called forth by God—"Reign of God," "Sovereignty of God," "God's Dream," "Messianic Age," "City of God," "Eschatological Family," "Dynasty of Spirit," and, yes, "Kingdom of God." These are all relatively apt terms to represent the concrete, broken and healed relationship we actually have with God in history.

## 6. THE REIGN OF GOD IN HISTORY

Recall what we aim to achieve in this chapter. We want to understand our relationship to God. We have already seen the double relationship, experienced on our part by the questions we have about both the world around us and the inner world that wonders, and on God's part by a double mission of Word and Spirit. We examined how that double relationship is broken through sin. Then we examined the symbols we use to represent this concrete, double, broken relationship in history. We concluded that a plurality of converging symbols works better than any one symbol.

Now, to complete the analysis of our relationship to God, we must set this symbolic representation within a *theology of history*. To avoid confusing you, the reader, I will usually use the term *Reign of God*. In English, at least, it does not connote the sexual exclusivity that Kingdom can, and it does connote more extension in time rather than the more geographic connotations of Kingdom. But I encourage you not to think of this term but rather of the divine, historical reality to which it or any of its cognates refer.

To grasp the *historical* character of the Reign of God, recall that the three diverging developments of the notion of Kingdom in the first few centuries of the Christian era possessed a power that the original, apocalyptic-eschatological use of the term did not. They were rooted in a philosophy and spoke to minds with philosophical questions. Therefore, because the good news was originally a statement about something historical and not sheerly about an afterlife, we ought to clarify in philosophical terms what early Christians probably took for granted about the nature of history itself.

Just as we have realized that a community is something over and above the individuals who make it up, so too history is something over and above the communities living it out. Now, "over and above" does not mean that communities are merely vehicles or functional aspects of a larger reality called history, any more than individuals lose their priority in the larger reality called community. It means rather that history is something that has a nature and a dynamic that is not reducible to a mere string of dynamics of communities. History is a reality that outlasts its communities just as each of its communities is a reality that outlasts its members. Human history has been alive for about five million years now, unfolding according to certain intelligible processes that will continue until the end of human time. History is worth our reflection and care, worth a solicitude and an appreciation that goes beyond care merely for our own friends and our own children.

The most obvious but most essential aspect of history is that *it flows;* that is, every historical event can in principle be completely explained by appeal to the historical events immediately preceding it. The flow is not predetermined in a way that skirts human freedom to obey or disobey the dictates of reason and conscience. But a chain of outcomes is intelligible in the sense that anyone's mind and heart can work only on that person's actual historical situation, including both the operative values in the community and one's own store of traditional wisdom.

The point here is that 99 percent of the meanings that shape our lives were shaped by our forebears, and what we do with these meanings will shape the lives of those who inherit our own legacy. In this perspective, we might suspend for a moment our commitment to the formula of an eternal Christ who "for us and for our salvation came down from heaven: by the power of the Holy Spirit he was born of the virgin Mary and became flesh." We enhance that truth if we regard Christ also as an Ancestor, a Forebear, who lived about sixty generations ago, whose words and deeds changed the meanings of the lives of his friends and thereby changed the flow of human history. He is a friend of a friend ... of a friend of ours, and our story about tomorrow will flow from the quality of our friendship with him today. This is the kind of belief in Christ that the early churches had long before they formulated any creeds in philosophical language.

Christ's role as a historical Forebear gives meaning not only to his future but also his past, in a process equally historical. When we think of Mother Teresa, we admire the work she does for the dying in Calcutta. There was a day, however, when she asked to be dispensed from her vows as a sister of Loretto—a day of sadness, no doubt, for her community and probably herself as well. Yet her future has redeemed her past, and we all know it. In this same way, the work of Jesus gave new meaning to the Testament we call "Old." So it is the nature of history that later events can give redemptive meaning to earlier ones. The word of God that history itself is, therefore, is a word of continual invitation to reinterpret the past in terms of the paschal mystery.

Since Jesus was a Jew preaching to Jews, the earliest conceptions of this Kingdom were strongly tinged with Jewish monarchical nationalism. But by the time of the death of Saint Paul, it seems to have dawned on all the major churches that God's plan of salvation was meant for the entire world. So we can identify this unity of history with this Kingdom of God. Even though it has been only through the preaching of Jesus of Nazareth that the race recognized God's kind purpose and named it a Kingdom, nevertheless, we have come to learn that the single will of God has always been a solidarity of humankind in time with significant enduring beyond all time.

Here I am trying to avoid theologies of history that describe God's activity as merely interruptive. God is not repeatedly fine-tuning a creation poorly designed from the start. Nor does God have a mere collection of individual vocations for individual persons. God has a single "will" to share the divine life with the human race as a unitary community. It is only in this perspective that any specific "will" of God for an individual can make any sense.

We are now in an excellent position to define the Reign of God (including any and all of its cognates) in terms related to the inner and outer Words of God in history.

*The Reign of God is the historical process of effective obedience to the divine pull in consciousness.*

Let me explain the terms of the definition. First, the Reign of God is a *process*. It is much better to think of the Reign of God this way than of some idealized socioreligious order. The Reign of God was certainly not the Constantinian "Christendom," nor will it ever be what some self-appointed "Christian Democratic" party could ever establish. Nor is the Reign of God to be identified with any church, unless, like Augustine, we redefine "church" as wherever men and women act in faith, hope, and charity. The point here is that the Reign of God is not a concept, not a plan. Nor is it any specific, identifiable community. It is a web of real events, where each event sets up a new historical situation out of which further events will develop.

The process we call Reign of God is *effective;* that is, the Reign of God includes not only the acts of inner obedience to God's good spirit working in people but also the results of that obedience in the social order. The Reign of God, therefore, includes interpretations of civil law, psychotherapies, diplomatic agreements, the handing on of tradition, and any other acts of creativity and consensus that sustain and nourish a culture. Likewise, it includes the moral standards and religious values that give a religion substance, as well as the tangible changes that happen to a community that applies those standards and values to its way of life.

In reality, of course, history is not a single, directly intelligible unity. The historical effects of that inner obedience do not eliminate the historical effects of inner disobedience. Wherever people know the good and refuse to do it, the coherence of history is torn apart. In other words, the diversions of the flow of history away from what makes sense occur wherever people refuse to obey their inner impulses to loving, responsible, reasonable, and intelligent living. History is scarred by wars and oppression, but it all begins in an inner disobedience to a divine pull in consciousness.

Thus, we must define the Reign of God as *historical;* but history is not the Reign of God. Rather, the Reign of God is a leaven within history. It is hidden, but it is a very real force in the flow of history. It has the power to deflate enmity, to unmask social myths, and to revive hope in spite

of the horrors of the past. Because of this blend of obedience
and disobedience, it is extremely difficult to tell where the
Reign of God is coming specifically. We can never say that
it arrives in this particular community and not in that. The
best we can muster is a conviction that at a specific time
and place we have obeyed the divine pull on our consciousness and made some creative contribution to history's
unfolding.

The Reign of God we long for will never come fully in
human history. The inner drift toward darkness tugs on us
all, progeny of original sinners that we are. So we imagine
the fullness of the Reign of God only in something beyond
history, in what we call an afterlife. Whatever that existence may be, and although descriptions are mostly fancy,
we can at least draw one conclusion from the truth that God
has irrevocably given his inner and outer Word to humanity:
*The fullness of God's Reign is eternally historical.* Let me
explain.

The humanity that Jesus embraced was not simply an
isolated nature of an individual, isolatable "person." In
being one individual he embraced the entirety of the human
race—not by an unintelligible divine decree but through the
historical interconnections by which any individual becomes
fully human by making his or her meaning felt in history.
For all of us, being a human means being interconnected.

Likewise, the gift of God's spirit within us is not only
for our individual salvation but also for the historical community of which we are a part. It is the nature of God
within us to overflow in love of those around us. God's self-
gift in us is essentially the power to give ourselves in love
to others.

We can expect, therefore, that the fullness of the Reign
of God will not abrogate history at all. On the contrary, the
Reign of God will make history brilliantly perfect. The New
Jerusalem will come down from God out of heaven, prepared
as a bride adorned for her husband (Rv 21:2). In whatever
sense we remain human in an "afterlife," we remain histor-

ical and interconnected in a manner by which all the ambiguities that surround our lives on earth will be resolved once and for all. All the genuinely loving and responsible connections we have made to others will finalize the persons we have become and be identical to the glory of God.

This is God's dream. When we make any decision about our lives, we are not merely responsible for what we are making of ourselves as individuals. We are breaking and making relationships that have eternal meaning for the Reign that God desires. Therefore, the decision of a retreat is a liberating praxis to let God's Dream be our own.

# CHAPTER FOUR

---

# The Image of History

What concretely is the work of the Reign of God? What do you thank God for as you lay down at night? How are we to understand the different views of "church" contained in the various New Testament books? Is a bishop a good bishop because he runs a smooth operation? Puts all his trust in God? Has progressive programming?

Do you have the peace you expect from life? When do we work to avoid trouble and when to accept the cross? By what measure do we say the family is doing fine?

In answering each of these questions, we spontaneously use some image of what "good" ought to mean. We then use that image as a lamp to guide us in making "good" decisions. The problem is, we do this without even noticing the powerful effect that this background image imposes on our consciousness.

These images represent for us, long before we analyze it, the work of finding and putting meaning into the history we are part of. Prior to naming that work as God's Reign or salvation or healing or peace, we represent it through images drawn from everyday experience. Even before we designate some liturgical or artistic symbol to represent what transcendence means for today, we use a more primary inner image to guide our symbol making.

The manner in which we envision bringing about anything good imposes a fundamental shape upon our entire consciousness. It restricts what we pay attention to, making us partly blind and partly perceptive. It confines and channels our problem-solving and creative abilities. What is most important for a person making a decision is to name his or her image of order. Our image of order preselects, as it were, the options we more consciously select for deliberation.

To liberate our consciousness we need a grammar of images. Having a language to deal with our preconscious image of order will help us widen our perspectives. Most important, we can more directly address the ungodly and destructive images of order that surround us today and take a conscious stand on an image that is both a sound philosophy and a faithful bearer of the paschal mystery of life that God has revealed through Jesus and the Spirit.

## 1. A PROCESS IMAGE

I must point out here that the images I am talking about are not goal images—not images of the ideal community or the anticipated results of some five-year plan. Rather, they are process images, that is, images of the work involved in steering history. It is the difference between a description of an island one is sailing toward and a description of the art of sailing.

The difference between these two kinds of images struck me forcefully when I realized that the goal images of Ignatius of Loyola changed rather often during his lifetime, but that his process image of the work of salvation remained constant. Since the earliest days after his conversion, he saw that salvation, or the spiritual life, was a struggle between the inner pull to pride and the inner pull to humility.

The same may be said, I believe, of Jesus himself. Although he left no account of his own self-reflections, he clearly shifted his goals during his public life. He began by preaching repentance, but many did not repent. He healed, but many never thanked God for what had happened to them. He gathered a community of faithful followers, but they did not understand what he was about. One after another, each of his goals failed him. And yet he is consistently portrayed as struggling against an enemy within people.

It seems to me, then, that the true charism of a religious leader will be found in how he or she conceives the work of God's Reign. Therefore, being consistent with our intention to name the conscious acts that constitute spiritual realities, we ought to express that work of God's Reign in terms verifiable in everyone's inner experience.

What are these process images? They are not mental photographs, mere graphical forms one could draw. Rather, they are remembered dramas—sequences of experiences one remembers from inherited stories or from one's own life. For example, suppose a mother regards her work in raising children essentially as protection. The guiding image in her mind is neither a concept nor a picture of protection; it is rather her memory of protecting and being protected, of childhood house play, of fairy tales, and of family lore about grandparents.

If it is memories that make up our image of the work of bringing about God's salvation, we face the question of how to distinguish in ourselves which memories are normative and which are not. Moreover, we need a way to assess these same process images in others, since people vary widely in their approaches to life.

When we do raise the question of our approaches to life, we usually talk about "models." It is common today to hear the question, What model are you using? The question has generated a thousand articles and a million discussions. The idea that we use models to shape our thinking dominates not only ecclesiology and spirituality but also the sciences of sociology, psychology, and economics. For a while model making was helpful because it allowed us to ask about the nonconceptual presuppositions that underlie the differences between people. But now that the issue of models is out on the table, it has become a point of honor never even to hint that someone else's model of church or image of redemption leaves something to be desired. Criticizing someone else's model risks being countercharged with something like, "Oh, you're coming out of the historical-critical model, aren't you?"—as if no models can be grounded in anything but their mere right to exist in somebody's mind.

This problem of the relativity of models, where yours is just as acceptable as mine, needs to be addressed. I suspect that few people really believe that one model is as good as another. They simply have no rational way of criticizing any-one else's approach to life, and so they are left with a benign tolerance by default. Particularly in matters of a person's own memories as the store of images defining transcend-ence, we trespass on very private grounds. Yet even though we keep our mouths politely shut, we do make judgments on the way others go about things. We mutely assess others' memories of what works in life, just as they quietly assess ours. The problem is how to put this critique into words that make a fruitful dialog possible.

Our question, therefore, is this: What words best rep-resent the different ways we remember putting order into life?

## 2. FOUR WAYS TO MAKE SENSE

Following again the seminal work of Bernard Lonergan in his book *Insight*,[1] we find that we experience insights in four fundamental ways. Before describing these in detail, let me say that each type of insight depends on an image, and therefore that there will be four basic kinds of images that represent the understanding essential to the process of making good choices in life. After we have looked at each kind of image, we should have a clear idea of both the power of certain images and their inability to represent our high-est aspirations.

What are these four kinds of insight? In what Lonergan calls the *classical* (alluding to the kind gained in the "classical" physics of Newton and Galileo), we have a simple if-then understanding of the relationship between events. Where there's smoke, there's fire. When I turn this switch, the light goes on. We anticipate these direct, routine relationships all the time. We expect the sun to rise in the morning, the toaster to pop, the newspaper to be delivered. This expectation works not as a deduction from a metaphysics but first and foremost as an image in consciousness. We can find its prime analogy in our experience of the sun's rising and setting, the regular alternation of night and day, although as an image it is easily associated with any sort of regularity whatsoever.

The second kind of insight is called *statistical*. Here we grasp that there is no direct functional relationship between certain kinds of events. Cancer is no respecter of persons. Rainfall has nothing to do with state boundaries. Just as we sometimes expect regularity, so at other times we expect coincidences and surprises. We deal with these randomly connected events not by formulating a set of if-then relationships but by setting a norm and seeing whether the deviations from the norm have any pattern. If they do, we suspect something of the classical order at work. If my uncle consistently gets better poker hands than I do, I suspect he is relying on more than the random fall of the cards. We find prime analogies for the coincidental in our experience of a bolt of lightning, of running into someone unexpectedly, or of discovering beauty in the play of light and shadow under a tree.

Now, the classical and the statistical expectations have to do with specific events. The following two further ways focus on how certain events develop out of others—in other words, on the chain of unrepeated events.

We experience a *genetic* kind of insight when we understand a predetermined pattern of growth. For example, Erik Erikson describes our psychological development as an alternating sequence of crisis and resolution, where the resolution of, say, the crisis of identity creates the materials for the further crisis of intimacy, and so on. On the more commonplace level, we all understand that our plants need rich dirt and fresh water to grow. People need the regular application of TLC to grow. What the sun does for a classical expectation or lightning does for statistical expectation, these commonplace experiences of growth do for a genetic expectation. A genetic expectation assumes that growth is natural. It follows a law we can depend on. The driver of the development, be it regular watering or an alternating pattern of crisis and resolution, remains the same, while the thing being driven really does change.

Finally, we have a *dialectical* kind of insight when we see that there is no definite sequence of events that governs growth. Probably the most familiar example of this is the flowering of human friendship. But unlike the flowers from our gardens, the blossoming of friendship is unpredictable. Its growth does not follow any fixed genetic sequence. As we all know, the friendship makes the friends just as much as friends make the friendship. This is because the drivers of dialectical development—in this case the friends themselves—are themselves changed in the growth process. Not that friendships do not have classical, statistical, and genetic factors as a kind of infrastructure, but to understand a particular marriage or love affair, we get a lot further by talking about its actual history, with its sudden turns and the unexpected shifts in attitudes that each partner took, than by jamming it into such classical frameworks as "a dependency relationship" or "a parent-child relationship" or "henpecked."

These four kinds of insight form a basic and relatively closed set of intellectual occurrences. Single events are either directly intelligible or they are not, and sequences of events are either directly intelligible or they are not. So, as far as grounding images is concerned, we have a good base to start from.

Our next question, then, is, What sort of images correspond to these kinds of insight? Keep in mind that by "image" we do not mean something geometric, or even a static picture of, say, a tree or a thunderstorm. Primarily the image is a memory of some recognizable human experience of change, which only subsequently is named, narrated, and explained.

## 3. FOUR PROCESS IMAGES

1. The first image is rooted in the classical intelligibility found in the regular, dependable appearance of sun and moon. Let me call it the *preservative* image, in which life is stable and enduring because its seasons are predictable and cyclic. A person feels at ease if the present is a smooth continuation of the past and gets the jitters when the unexpected breaks in. The best future will be an icon of the past, with its warm hearth and convivial supper table. Although a geometric representation of this image may be a circle, the cosmological image of the sun or the seasons certainly makes itself felt in consciousness more deeply.

In the preservative image, one person's authority over another is legitimated not by mere force of personality, which escapes rational explanation, but by some kind of contract—if only as natural as parenthood—in which the parties agree to a set of if-then conditions. This synchronizes their interpersonal harmony with the apparent harmonies of the universe. Typically, its authority is hierarchical, just as its Aristotelian cosmology is hierarchical, with the prime movers resting far from this little center of chaos we call home. It is an image by which the rationality of the whole must govern every part. As such, it is oblivious to idiosyncrasies and intolerant of any exceptions to the rule.

The preservative image also reaches into the depths of a person's psyche. The ordered soul is the soul that remembers what it was taught and pays little attention to the dreams and fantasies that bubble to the surface now and then. It is not unadaptable, but adaptation is conceived as putting the traditional message in a modern dress, as if there could be no real need for new, unheralded meanings. Thinking, therefore, is a matter of applying principles, bringing the wisdom of the past to bear on the present. Any failure to meet some crisis is due not to the newness of the crisis, for there are no completely new crises, but to our own shortsightedness.

We can see this kind of image in Matthew's Gospel.[2] His church was in danger of breaking apart. The destruction of Jerusalem in A.D. 70 prompted Matthew's church and the Pharisee party each to close ranks, with each side forbidding anyone to belong to the other. Consequently, the Matthean church needed some touchstone of belonging that was not racial, for it included both Jews and Greeks, nor merely liturgical, for the Christian liturgies were almost completely derived from the Jewish. Matthew's church was also shaken from within by the teachings of some false prophets. Dissension was rising and charity was growing cold. They also needed a principle of discernment with which to test the spirits.

To find a source of identity and a criterion of discernment, they looked to the teachings of Jesus and to the authorities whom Jesus appointed to lead. It was a community governed by word and rulers rather than spirit and populace. The Sermon on the Mount was its Magna Charta, which Jesus concluded with an injunction to test prophets by their fruits, presumably whether or not they act according to the Sermon they have just heard. Jesus gave Peter the keys to the Kingdom and the jurisdictional power to "bind and loose." Matthew has no Pentecost. It is not the Spirit who will guide the church but Jesus. Where Jesus exorcises demons in the power of the Spirit, the disciples do so in the name of Jesus. Matthew concludes his Gospel with the words "teach them to observe all the *commands I gave* you, and know that *I* am with you always; yes, to the end of time."

2. The second kind of image is linked to our insight into coincidences. Whether or not these insights are correct is beside the point. Right or wrong, we name certain conjunctions lucky or unlucky. Call it the *interruptive* image. In this perspective life is full of surprises, but all ultimately trustworthy. The person who lives best is the trusting person, allowing unexpected possibilities and asking for no more than one's daily bread. Even in unfortunate accidents there is no use railing against the gods. It's either just an accident or else the gods are interrupting our lives for no apparent reason. Where the preservative image anticipates a circular kind of order, this interruptive image expects a vertical bolt out of the blue.

Life is full of interruptions, and we must give them their due. Better an anarchical social order that responds to the peculiarities of individuals than a hierarchical one that ignores them. The interruptive expectation is an agnostic image insofar as it denies our ambitions to control our lives and so downplays setting goals and making long-range plans. This is often the attitude of the very poor or wounded, admirable in their readiness to take one day at a time, but in most cases having little alternative. We see it also in a Mother Teresa or a Jean Vanier, who identify so closely with the wounded in our world.

The most important spiritual relationships are vertical, ready to respond to God's interruption of the human drama. The present moment is a sacrament, of infinite worth though it last but a moment. Spiritual freedom means "letting go and letting God." Horizontal relationships may be short-term or not, but they are often quite intimate and poignant.

In the Scriptures, John's Gospel reveals such an image. Think of the timeless conversations Jesus had with Nicodemus at night or with the woman at the well. Think of how

Jesus seems to have wandered suddenly into the lives of the man born blind and of the sick man at the Pool of Bethzatha. Think of his response to Mary at Cana that his "hour had not yet come" and then the wonderful surprise of the best wine last. Or recall his response to Martha's hope in a far-off resurrection: "I am the Resurrection," he says, cutting through her notions of future and focusing her gaze only on him. To see him, John says, is already to see the Father. I believe that we cannot really fathom the enigmatic statements in John about Jesus being in the Father and vice versa unless we locate them in the context of John's bolt-out-of-the-blue vision of how this world gets its meaning.

Authority in the Johannine church is not by ordination or appointment. There are no "apostles." Except for two pericopes that mention "the twelve," there is no designated *office* of discipleship. The primacy of discipleship is held by Mary Magdalene and the Beloved Disciple, simply because they love Jesus. They reached out to him physically; they stood by him at the cross; they were the first to believe in the Resurrection. Nor is there any missionary activity. John's church is a sectarian, inner-directed community of love. It is guided by the Spirit, a Spirit of forgiveness: "Receive the Holy Spirit; whose sins you shall forgive. . . ." God's Spirit is a wind, Jesus says, "that blows where it wills; you cannot tell where it comes from or where it is going; and so it is with all who are born of the spirit."

3. Our third type of vision may be called *progressive*. It draws its image and power from our insights into the natural growth of flowers, trees, and animals, including ourselves. There is plenty of evidence around us and within us that life has a natural power to expand and progress, almost as if we can do little to stop it. It is an optimistic view, of course, although it also accounts for the dying of things as equally natural. It differs from the preservative expectation because it loathes stagnation or mere repetition. In a preservative culture, such as Ireland's, they say, "You've never

seen anything like it" as a warning. In a progressive culture, such as North America's, we say it to sell refrigerators.

To monitor the meaningfulness of life authorities must
be farmers, preparing the ground but letting the seeds
sprout under their own power. The farmer may have been
appointed or just someone with a green thumb. What counts
is the ability to foster growth. Governance is a matter of
fertilizing, using fences to define specific but ample outer
limits within which the governed may grow as they please.
The greatest crimes are child abuse, teaching nonsense, and
polluting the environment—whatever prevents nature and
spirit from their natural blossoming.

To catch the image of the spirituality of the progressive
image, imagine that everything is a door to something better. You wake each morning in the hope of improving something, becoming a better person, leaving the world a better
place. What counts is not obedience to external laws, which
to some extent you can wink at, but obedience to the inner
urgings of the creative spirit.

Luke's Gospel and his Acts of the Apostles seem shaped
by such a progressive image. In contrast to Matthew's preservative image, which relies on provincial authority to define membership, and to John's anarchical image of a closed
sect, Luke looks to all of humanity. His genealogy of Jesus
begins not from Abraham but from Adam, making Christ
to be the New Adam, in whom all humanity finds its liberation. The Holy Spirit moves quietly in the conception of
Jesus and in those who welcome this child, like a seed of
God planted and waiting to break upward. And when it fully
breaks at Pentecost, it speaks all the languages of humanity, as a wonderful pledge to end the curse of Babel. Christianity seems to burst forth, even from the unpromising turf
of the Gentiles, spreading like myrtle across Asia Minor to
Rome, with the promise that it will reach even to "the ends
of the earth."

Where Matthew suppresses mention of the Holy Spirit
in favor of an ordination by Jesus, Luke makes Pentecost

the ordination of the apostles and the long-expected sign that the Day of Yahweh has come. In Peter's Pentecostal address he cites the prophet Joel: "It shall come to pass in the last days, says God, that I will pour out a portion of my spirit on all humanity. Your sons and daughters shall prophesy. Your youngsters shall see visions and your old shall dream dreams. Yes, even on my servants and handmaids I will pour out a portion of my spirit in those days and they shall prophesy." From then on, it is clearly the Holy Spirit who guides the church, and, where the Spirit has come upon anyone, the apostles must baptize them.

4. Finally there is a *dialectical* expectation, born of our sobering experiences of malice and stupidity and of our struggles to overcome them, principally in ourselves. In contrast to the preservative, interruptive, and progressive images, which draw their analogies from nature, the dialectical image draws upon human experience itself. Geometrically, the image may be a line with arrowheads on each end pulling in opposite directions, but, again, the psychological experience of interpersonal tension cuts much deeper. In our families, our occupations, our churches, our friendships, at every turn of events, the participants themselves change to some extent, making future turns of events difficult to predict.

But social groupings are not the prime analogy. The dialectics *between* people can be clarified by looking at the dialectics *within* people. We can see this if we consider our own history of dealing with our emotions. At best, the intelligent thing for us to do is to recognize our feelings, and the responsible thing to do is to decide whether to trust them or not. But none of us does this very well. We repress some feelings and indulge others. And, having done that, we habituate our intelligence as well as our feelings to continue in the same style, making some of us uptight, some gushy, some bizarre, and some boring. Our affectivities and our intellects have conditioned each other, defined each other's

limits through the actual life choices we have made, not
because we have explicitly chosen one series of *objects* over
another, but because we have implicitly chosen one deploy-
ment of our *subjectivity* over another.

While we all know this at one level of awareness, not
all of us view humanity chiefly in these terms. For example,
a psychological counselor with the progressive mindset acts
as though our problems all stem from the unfertile soil of
an unhappy family or from being choked by the thorns of
some anxiety. A counselor with the dialectical expectation
acknowledges these environmental factors but looks also to
the dialectical possibilities of the human soul. Where we
have been malicious, there is also a therapy of repentance,
forgiveness, and reconciliation. Where we have been dull of
spirit, there is also a therapy of understanding exactly how
the dialectics in our life experiences have deformed our
minds and hearts, followed by an envisioning of healthier
alternatives.

Mark's Gospel shows many of these features. Immediately after his baptism, Jesus is thrust by the force of the
Holy Spirit into a wilderness inhabited by wild beasts, there
to open the long-awaited battle against Satan while being
looked after by angels. After this opening sally Jesus' first
and primordial miracle is an exorcism, which amounts to a
proclamation that the nature of his mission is to defeat the
Evil Spirit that has defeated his brothers and sisters. While
the disciples have to struggle to understand who Jesus is
and what he is about, the demons know immediately who
he is. He is Son of the Most High God, and he has come to
destroy them. He calls the legalistic traps of the Pharisees
"temptations." He will describe himself as a robber who
breaks into Satan's house, ties him up, and plunders his
property.

But the destruction of the powers of evil cannot be accomplished in a single victory. The Jesus of Mark groans in
spirit, laments the obtuseness of his disciples, is indignant
when they push children away, twice lays hands on a blind

man to complete a cure, calms a storm, calms another storm, warns about coming disasters, curses a barren tree, kicks over money tables—here is a contentious Saviour! Immediately after Peter first acknowledges that Jesus is the Christ, Jesus jarringly makes the first of three predictions of his death. The narrative culminates in his greatest act of ministry—neither a profound teaching, nor a healing, nor even an exorcism, in fact no miracle at all. It is his martyrdom on the cross. At the cross itself a Roman centurion recognizes that "truly this was the Son of God" by witnessing the way Jesus struggled unto death.

Have I have too neatly found four Gospels corresponding to four expectations of what "order" means in the world? Perhaps. Certainly the Evangelists did not intend to canonize any particular view of the soul's struggle. Nor are the differences between them as stark as I may have made them. Still, it is not difficult to find in other books of the Bible one of these four images of transcendence shaping its vision. Perhaps the reason we have many books in The Book is precisely because the human spirit needed the full range of world images within which to hear the good news.

In any case, the four Gospels do convey four images of order, willy-nilly. Although Scripture does not discuss images as such, it is still a kind of "code," as Northrop Frye has suggested, which shapes the language and preconscious expectations of successive cultures, in a manner quite independent of the depth of their faith in God. It should come as no surprise, therefore, that the heuristic codes embedded in the Scriptures would resonate with the heuristic possibilities of every person's imagination.

If you have detected in my analysis a preference for the dialectical kind of image of the soul's work, you have anticipated correctly. The dialectical draws its analogy directly from human experience itself, while the other three draw their analogies from the stars, the weather, and the fields. As such, by themselves alone they cannot adequately rep-

resent the phenomenon of disobedience to our own nature—
an irrationality found only in creatures such as we.

Also, I do not mean to dismiss Matthew, Luke, and John
simply because of the very general, albeit forceful, impression they give about what kind of spiritual insights are
needed in the unfolding of the Reign of God. If the Gospels
are expansions on the core story of Jesus' death and resurrection, these evangelists certainly intended to convey to
their hearers the principle of life-through-death, the principle that it is better to suffer evil than to do it, and the
principle that the real evils of the world crop up in the human heart—all of which the image of the cross is meant to
represent in compact form.

Nor do I wish to canonize Mark's contentious vision of
salvation. In our history the image of struggle has too
quickly been associated with a Manichaean objectification
of inner experience into two absolute and opposing forces of
Good and Evil. What is worse, a misunderstanding of the
nature of the inner struggle has repeatedly been associated
with mere struggle between two groups of people, which
unfortunately has often been construed as God's permission
to slaughter any group deemed non-Christian.

Yet, considered precisely as an image of the work of the
soul, the inner struggle between good and evil tendencies
represents the finest moments in our tradition. If we are
going to assist people in making good decisions, it will help
if we can set that work into the historical context of what
has been going forward ever since Abraham left Ur of the
Chaldees.

## 4. HISTORY OF THE DIALECTICAL IMAGE

With more or less emphasis on preservative, interruptive, and progressive images, the Bible shows a gradual
emergence and eventual dominance of a dialectical image of
salvation. From the time of Abraham, Israel broke away

from the preservative cosmology of a circular time frame into a progressive time frame. True, the Torah is preservative in character, but it is embedded in the promise of a land flowing with milk and honey. But Israel's awareness of time was also interruptive. As history unfolded, Israel's calamities and infidelities cried out for God's interventions, through miraculous deeds in the desert and through the outcries of the prophets.

Finally, the good news of God-among-us proclaimed "a message which was a mystery," Paul says, "hidden for generations and centuries and has now been revealed to his saints. This mystery is Christ *among* you, your hope of glory. This is the Christ we proclaim, this is the wisdom in which we thoroughly train everyone and instruct everyone, to make them all perfect in Christ. It is for this I struggle wearily on, helped only by his power driving me irresistibly" (Col 1:27–29).

Here begins the dialectical image, in which God becomes carnal to accompany humanity, not to stand above it. As a driver of change, the Incarnate Word himself is changed. The godly life is depicted as an ongoing struggle unto death and the continuance of that paschal mystery forward in the generations of disciples to follow. The godly Spirit, living in everyone, groans in a great, continuous act of childbirth.

The dialectical consciousness grew quite slowly, however. The first inklings that a vision of present struggles was needed were felt as the churches became aware that the Parousia was not imminent. (If we are not looking forward to the end of time soon, what is time now?) The churches then began to reflect directly on the connection that our inner dialectics have to the grand-scale course of history. Paul described the war of flesh against spirit. The Desert Fathers offered ways to wage that war. Augustine fashioned a complete image of how the dialectic of the soul is identical to the very dialectic of history. In his work *On the Christian Combat*, he pits the love of God and neighbor against concupiscence, with its predilections for the world, the flesh, and the devil. Then in his *City of God*,[3] to explain the entire history of the world, reaching back to creation and the Fall of the Angels, and forward to the Bliss of Eternal life, he pits charity against what he calls "the lust to dominate."

A millennium later, Ignatius of Loyola, influenced by Augustine's theology of history, envisioned the world as a battleground between "the Commander-in-Chief of all Good People," Christ, and the Rebel Bandit, Lucifer. In his meditation "The Two Standards,"[4] Ignatius pits humility against pride, as Augustine did, but he adds the strategies by which Christ and Lucifer lead us one way or the other. Lucifer draws us to pride by tempting us first to dream about getting rich, then about being honored, and finally to pride. "From these three steps," he says, "the Evil One leads to all the other vices." Christ's strategy is the opposite, step for step. First we are drawn to desire poverty, at least spiritual if not actual; then to want to bear insults in imitation of Christ rather than honors; from these spring humility and, he says, "all other virtues."

Unfortunately, while the visions of Augustine and Ignatius sanctioned an interruptive and a dialectical imagination for Christianity, which was accompanied by a Ptolemaic cosmology reinforcing the preservative imagination, the only place for a progressive imagination in the church lay in the theories of automatic historical progress of Joachim of Fiore, which were condemned by council and scholastics alike. Then, beginning with Hegel, Marx, and the successes of the natural sciences, the idea of progress returned in secular dress. The Western imagination burned with the vision that history, despite its ups and downs, simply must make progress in the long run.

Such theories of *automatic* progress, in which history unfolds according to suprahistorical forces beyond the control of individual purposes, are neither confirmed nor denied by secular minds today. Government leaders and social philosophers tend to be much more practical and materialistic

in their thinking. Yet even though secular materialism es-
chews theories of inevitable progress, insofar as it dismisses
malice as a real factor in history, it embraces a progressive
vision of what consciousness must do to keep building something bigger and better. Perhaps two world wars and a
global truce based on stockpiling explosives have chilled any
progressive optimism of philosophers. They have certainly
not dampened the expectations of global corporations and
the superpowers that a better future is within the grasp of
any opportunist. They do not believe progress is automatic
at all. They rely on practical insight into situations to make
things better to the exclusion of any dialectical suspicion of
what "better" really means. If the Middle Ages were dialectical without the complement of progress, the twentieth
century has been progressive without the complement of
dialectics.

Meanwhile, the interruptive vision has kept popping up
over the centuries among fundamentalist or messianic
groups as a regular reaction to the complexity and perhaps
novelty of the progressive and dialectical visions of the soul's
work. It is today, as ever, the image of those who love the
simple solution. It easily allies itself with a preservative vision that maintains a strict social code of behavior. What
the preservative and interruptive kinds of images have in
common, linked as they are with insights into situations
and not into a *series* of situations, is an inability to imagine
historical development.

If Christians today are not much aware of this tradition
of a dialectical imagination, it is partly because the emergence of empirical method in science has left the parables
of Augustine and Ignatius shining their light in the wrong
corner. For all their power to stir up virtue in our hearts,
their parables do not give a functional explanation of *how*
loving God and neighbor and imitating Christ make a positive contribution to the social, historical order. But our culture today demands *functional understanding,* not mere
homilies or contemplations or ideals. If Christians today

must speak of such unverifiable entities as angels and dev-
ils, at least they should complement that mythical language
with empirical references to the processes of consciousness.
Likewise, if we are to practice virtue, we want to know what
good our virtue is for this world, not just the next; for our
neighbor, not just ourselves. Christians today want religion
to be more than a haven for troubled souls; they want it also
to be a creative force in secular society, offering alternatives
to human self-destruction that make sense to the secular
mind.

Another reason why the dialectical imagination has yet
to take hold of Christian consciousness is that it is easily
confused with an adversarial view of life. As we saw earlier,
it is not only self-centered individuals that account for sin
in the world; communities themselves have a self-centeredness reinforced by the very group affection that can convert
the self-centered member. It takes a strong dose of humility,
plus the ability to notice one's inner experiences, to see that
the tensions between people are essentially tensions within
people. It will take an astute Christian theory of power to
link this dialectical kind of spiritual insight with the economic and political processes that shape today's world.

## 5. CONVERSION OF THE IMAGINATION

If we are to tap our full creative powers, if we are even
to make a well-grounded decision in life, our imaginations
must be converted to expect any combination of the four
basic ways of responding to situations: preservative, interruptive, progressive, and dialectical, with dialectical holding
the dominant position. It is not enough to acknowledge simply that the human mind functions in this fashion. Unless
we test our own imaginations as they work on concrete problems, and unless we critique our imaginations to see
whether or not they include the dialectic of pull and coun-
terpull in their purview, our image of what history is about

will filter out some of the most important questions we can ask.

Let me give an example. Recently I heard of a discussion about the ethical use of fetal tissue to treat Parkinson's disease in the elderly. Both those who would ban the practice and those who would allow it focused on the dignity of the human person—of the fetus in the one case and of the elderly person in the other. It seemed as though opposite conclusions could be drawn from the same high principle. Then one woman piped up, "What I want to know is who is going to decide whose tissue gets used!" Suddenly the discussion dropped out of the classical, deductive mode of imagining the problem and into the dialectical mode. Real men and women, real parents, doctors, and lawyers walked into the picture. Now the question of the concrete dialectic of greed and selfishness versus responsibility and compassion stood out in everyone's mind. My point is not to argue for a particular ethical stance here; it is to argue for a way of imagining human problems.

For another example, we might compare the different ways each of us imagines what "peacemaking" involves. Some picture it as establishing the harmony of routine. Some focus on an utter trust in God's interventive care. For others it means unleashing our natural powers. And for still others it means a quality of consciousness that acts as umpire in the heart, scrutinizing inner events to call some "safe" and others "out." Again, my point is not to dismiss the values of routine, of trust, and of creativity; it is to highlight the role of the tensions in human consciousness in establishing those routines, trusting in that God, and exercising that creativity.

What is involved in converting our imaginations to a dialectical attitude? First, great care must be taken that our image of the dialectical nature of history is related to human hearts, not to human groups. Two of our traditional dialectical images of life, the image of the journey and the image of the battle, while they have the power to represent the soul's real work, can also be easily misinterpreted as struggles against other people who do not share our own holy desires and high ideals. "They do not walk with us on our journey!" "Onward Christian Soldiers!" These pious emblems then become just an imaginal rationalization for hating one's enemies.

Second, we should grow accustomed to realizing that everything has a history. Just as the flow of a river unerringly follows the laws of physics, so the flow of history follows the laws of dialectical intelligibility. Every bend in the river, every slight ripple, affects the entire flow downstream. The "downstream" of history, however, includes not only the succession of communal situations but the very resources of authenticity or unauthenticity of the community's members.

Human situations, therefore, cannot be explained by deductive reasoning alone, still less by statistics alone, and certainly not by some innate laws of growth. We must think on the level of history. An acquaintance who was being interviewed for the job of principal at a high school was asked, "What would you do if your assistant principal refused to handle discipline problems?" Rather than respond with some ready-made solution learned in some crisis-management workshop, he said, "I would be very anxious to find out the history of the situation."

Third, a dialectical imagination about life will therefore also expect every person to be a wounded person. We are all wounded simply by having to cope with situations we walked into or were born into. And we are wounded by our very inept attempts at surviving the pressures of life. What we see as we watch people on the street is a great troop of war veterans. What we might guage as poor performance is often a better performance than we could muster had we fought their battles. Those we might have called losers may actually be winning a very difficult and protracted campaign.

Fourth, a dialectical expectation will anticipate evil as well as grace. It envisions the entire pool of human resources as being constantly drained to water the petty egoisms of individuals and groups. Yet every person is responsible for her or his soul and ultimately responsible for history. Every person also has access to the grace of God. Let love flow to God and neighbor, dam up the channels that feed merely our security and reputation, and not only will our antagonisms be healed but there will flow forth a love from us that is full of creativity and invention for the good of the world around us.

Finally, a dialectical image of world process ought to uncover and repudiate the various versions of preservative, interruptive, and progressive worldviews with which it often competes. In the nineteenth century the idea of progress, spawned by the success of the natural sciences, dominated commonsense views of what makes life good. It was replaced in the twentieth century by the idea of community, which even today encompasses two rather divergent ideals—a preservative ideal and an interruptive ideal. The proponents of the preservative community tend toward totalitarianism, and these can be found not only in high government but in high churches as well. The proponents of the interruptive community tend toward sectarianism, extreme anti-government sentiments, and a withdrawal from history.

These ideals are still very much alive today. No day goes by that we do not feel their myopic forces on our psyches. If we fail to give our imaginations the full range of the mind's capacities (that is, of the fourfold battery of insights), we filter the psychic material we draw upon for creative thinking. In raising our children and in assessing public morals, we disagree on whether a situation is peaceful enough or not and on the kinds of remedies needed. In our personal lives we can actually hate the dialectical "unpeace" of our souls and cling to the false security of a merely preservative, interruptive, or progressive image.

In any case, if human beings are involved, we cannot leave the dialectical image out of the picture. We humans are in fact continually assailed by desires to dominate oth-

ers, to live a life dependent on no one, and to spend our
energies making a name for ourselves. To the degree that
these energies are shunted away from caring for others
and lavished on ourselves, the intellectual resources of
our culture go untapped and with each successive generation dry up.

No doubt there are equally great dangers at the opposite extreme. I am thinking of people who see life as nothing
but a continuous struggle. They can completely devalue any
enterprise that is not strictly dialectical; they can despair
of any benefit arising from the discipline of routine, ultimate
trust in God's providence, and optimistic hope for a better
future.

The challenge is to allow the dialectical image to stand
guard, as it were, over the preservative, interruptive, and
progressive energies as they are applied to life situations. If
our image of reality is exclusively preservative or interruptive or progressive, we are losing a war we deny is being
waged. We rationalize the terrors of history—genocide, mass
deportation, nuclear stockpiling, global hunger—not by
some theory but by imagining them as beyond the control of
human creativity. The progressive image deems the endless
civil war in Ireland as just "part of the scheme of things."
The interruptive image deems AIDS as just an "act of God."
The progressive image deems leveling a slum as just "the
price of progress." By failing to imagine the roots of all
things human as extending down into the recesses of consciousness to two contrary loves, we abdicate responsibility;
we mummify creativity.

King Solomon was considered wise because he asked
God not for some inner rule he could apply repeatedly to
create civil harmony nor for some radical trust in God's interventive care nor for a spirit of creativity that would ensure a continuously developing kingdom. He asked for a
discerning heart—a heart that knew how to test the claims
of two mothers over one child, two loves over one person. We
need such a heart today. I mean a heart that does more than

listen to the voices of conscience. I mean a heart that also looks at our own imaginations, to see whether or not they have the full, paschal breadth of a dialectical image of history.

# CHAPTER FIVE

---

# The Praxis of Noticing

In our reflection on human experience, history, and imagination, we have discovered a few basic structures—the inner and outer Words and the four typical images of historical process—within which we all make our choices. Let us now look more closely at how noticing, meditating, contemplating, and deliberating fit into that structure.

We begin with a few fundamental facts about noticing—so fundamental that you may be surprised to rediscover them.

## 1. PRINCIPLES

First: *We need to know what is going on if we are to live in the real world.* As a principle this seems obvious. Of course we have to know our situation before we can act on it. The reason for stating the principle here is that we often act without even trying to understand a situation. We might acknowledge the principle, but we lack the habit of mind, the praxis, of watching where we are going. Usually there is one specific area in our lives in which we repeatedly fail to know what is going on, blindly wrecking things that work in our favor and reinforcing things that do not. We have a blind spot. And the problem with blind spots is that we are unable to name or understand the area that we cannot look at.

In a retreat, where we step back to assess our relationships, we must expect to begin in ignorance. Ignorance, however, is a frightening state. It can scare us into grabbing the first—and usually the most simplistic—explanation of a reality that is somewhat complex. Particularly if we are accustomed to being on top of things, we will be impatient to put our skills to work before we fully understand what skills are needed.

Second: *We learn what is going on by posing questions to ourselves.* Suppose you are watching a television drama and you hear a phone ring. You wonder whether it is your own phone or the one on the TV program. Or suppose you wake up feeling depressed. Is it a low-pressure weather system outside or an emotional problem within? Or imagine that you read a letter from a friend that says, "I really enjoy every one of your letters." And you wonder, was that meant seriously or sarcastically?

To answer these spontaneous questions we naturally pose a further, more deliberately constructed question. Is the sound of the phone coming from the TV or from the hall? What is the weather like outside? Have I neglected writing my friend? If we cannot answer these questions easily, we may pose further deliberate questions until our initial question is answered.

Now, the reason for stating this principle is to explain what really makes the difference between people who usually know what is going on and those who usually do not. People who are oblivious to some reality around them are not literally blind, nor do they necessarily experience any different data coming in. The difference is that they do not pose deliberate questions to themselves, at least not about the reality at hand.

For most of us, who are partly oblivious and partly perceptive, it helps greatly to realize that we are not just looking at reality, seeing what is there to be seen. We are constructing possible explanations of what is going on by raising relevant questions. Becoming a perceptive person, then, means not just looking but letting our noticing arouse questions in us.

Third: *We pose deliberate questions to ourselves only if we have a genuine desire to know what is going on.* This principle explains why in certain areas we do not pose the further questions that lead to knowledge. We simply do not want to know.

There may be legitimate reasons for not wanting to know—"I don't care to answer the phone anyway, so why check to see if it's ringing?" Or the reasons may not be so legitimate—"Don't even suggest that my son might be taking drugs!" In any case, knowing what is going on depends far more on the will, the desire, the determination to live in reality than it does on mere intellectual powers. Some of the most perceptive people in the world may have immoral purposes for finding out the truth of a situation. But they clearly demonstrate how intelligent questions spring from a resolute desire to see how the land lies rather than from altruism and goodwill.

There are times when we believe we want to figure something out about our lives, but we discover an unnoticed resistance to the light. For example, we might suddenly discover that we have no desire to continue a retreat we have begun. Our desire to pray and reflect has vanished. This abrupt loss of interest is a clue that we may not want to learn about some relationship—to our spouse, children, job, self, or God. We are afraid to acknowledge a truth about our lives, so we suddenly feel a paralysis.

Usually it turns out that it is not the relationship itself we are afraid of. It is often the case that the relationship represents something very valuable to us but so vulnerable that we protect it with secrecy. In other words, we do not fear having the relationship to this person, this bottle, or this money; we fear losing what we believe that relationship gives us.

When we discover the existence of such a secret, before going any further in a retreat, it is important to acknowledge at least that there is a buried connection, some underground cable with the sign Do Not Dig Here. Simply to acknowledge its presence to another person, even without revealing its character, will raise for us the first, crucial, deliberative question, Why keep it hidden? Or, more to the point, Does this relationship give me something that I cannot do without and that I believe I cannot get elsewhere?

Fourth: *People who want to know what is going on have the habit of noticing.* The habit of noticing is something more than just experiencing. Two people can saunter through a museum and see the same paintings and yet notice very different things. World travelers do not necessarily know more about the world than those who stay at home; they learn more only if they wonder about the foreign lands and take note of clues, of evidence, of traces to ascertain what foreign people are like.

In contrast, people who want only to appear knowledgeable will not notice things. They will memorize. Their aim is to use knowledge to gain esteem from others. They have the annoying habit of being able to answer practically everything. They recite facts and give quick answers to anybody's questions about what happened and where, but they do not easily explain why or how things happened. We seldom hear them say, "I never noticed that!" or, "I wonder what this is for?" or, "That's curious!"

During a retreat it is important to remark about all kinds of things that strike us, at least to ourselves if not to a spiritual mentor. Many of the remarks may go nowhere, but the atmosphere of free noticing gives our psyches permission to call both our more tender and our more menacing memories out into the light. Not that we are trying to embarrass or frighten ourselves. We do not aim to *feel* something. We aim to *know* something. We are allowing data to surface in order to shape some key questions about our lives. Free noticing is fruitful when it puts us in a frame of mind that genuinely seeks the truth around us and within us.

Fifth: *The inner data of consciousness are just as important to notice as the data from the five senses.* A "situation," or what I have referred to as "what is going on," includes our own feelings, questions, observations, suspicions, beliefs, and commitments. The point of this principle is to underline the fact that we do not always know what we are feeling. We are unable to formulate a question we have. We cannot put our finger on what was important in a conversation we are convinced was important.

Many people are under the impression that since they experience these feelings, questions, and so on, they must know what they are. But inner experiences can be just as unrecognized as voices on a telephone. Have you ever noticed, for example, that you have been feeling angry and didn't realize it for some time? Or consider the times when someone's disagreement with you made you realize how tenaciously you have clung to a certain belief all your life. Even at this present moment is it not true that you are bothered by questions that you cannot put into words yet?

Being fully "objective," then, means noticing and questioning our own inner events as well as what we see, hear, smell, taste, and touch. It means taking the time to notice our own consciousness, like running a comb through the psyche looking for snarls. It means frequently turning our attention away from the objects of our worries, hopes, memories, and cares and turning instead to the inner events of worrying, hoping, remembering, and caring. Is it really worry that we are experiencing? Might it be fear? Is the experience connected to other similar experiences? Is the worry really warranted or just compulsive? Should I allow the worry to surface further questions?

Noticing inner experience with a view to questioning it is the essence of the art of discerning the spirits. And the key experience to notice in retreat is our love for God. Yet this love, even though it is alive in each one of us, is not immediately recognizable. We will treat this in more detail below.

Sixth: *The outer data of sense can reveal the inner data of consciousness.* When we notice someone acting strangely, we imagine what might be going on inside them—provided, of course, we have the habit of wondering about inner events. With others, of course, we have no direct access to their inner experience, only their words and their behavior. What is important to grow accustomed to, however, is that their behavior can belie their words. They may either be lying about how they feel or they may be making an honest mistake. "I feel fine!" is usually not true, but polite dissimulation is one thing and repression is another.

An excellent way to expect that people may be thinking and feeling things that they cannot admit is to discover ourselves doing it. For years I told people I would not want to work in a certain school. Yet the truth was I did want to work there but felt that circumstances prevented it. So rather than live with a lost hope, I let go of hope, let go so much that I believed what I was telling others. I discovered this inner hope when someone pointed out to me that I actually visited the school quite often.

Psychotherapists will use this technique of looking at behavior to help clients discover their own inner thoughts and feelings. To discover your own values, look at your phone bills. To find out your feelings about someone, recall exactly what you do with them. If there is someone you say you have a great affection for but do not talk to, "great affection" probably does not well represent your actual feelings and thoughts about that person. For those of us who have suppressed certain feelings for a long time—grief, anger, jealousy—the exercise reacquaints us with feelings that have become strangers in our house. In other words, by standing outside ourselves and watching our behavior from a distance, we can let insights arise about what this person—ourselves—may really be thinking and feeling.

Seventh: *Everything we know originated in somebody, somewhere, noticing something.* Granted, most of what any person knows is accepted on belief. As youngsters grow up they gradually test some of the beliefs and values of their parents, but they do so by noticing whether or not their own experience bears out what they have learned.

What many of us do not realize until much later in life is that noticing was necessary to discover the inherited truth or value in the first place. There are no divine messages that come out of the sky. There is only ourselves noticing something about our experiences, putting questions to ourselves, and realizing the truth about life. There may be logical ramifications and conclusions stemming from what we learned, but the first principles from which we deduce further truths were not themselves deduced. They were realized by someone with a desire to know and, most likely, with the habit of noticing.

True, Scripture does not portray the origins of religious knowledge as an inner construction like this. God talked to Moses from a burning bush. Saint Paul was knocked to the ground. Saint Matthew was told by Jesus "Follow me," and he followed. But much of this reporting owes its picturesque style to the relative inability of Israelites to explain inner experience. In its place are theophanies, dreams, angels, and voices from the sky. Whether or not God has discontinued the dramatic approach in our own times, there can be no doubt that Moses, Paul, and Matthew had already wanted to serve God in some way. They were intent on obeying God and alert to their own experience for any clues about how to do that. They paid attention not only to the signs of the times but to the stirrings of their own hearts as well. To discount their inner experience during these divine visitations is to deny the role of God's Spirit in welcoming the Word.

Before any knowledge of God came questions about God. Before any questions came noticing. Before noticing came a dark and relentless desire. It can come as a shock to realize this essential role of human noticing, questioning, and desire in divine revelation. But it is a healthy shock. We discover a profound camaraderie with all the men and women who seek the truth about life. We are engaged in the same struggle as they are. What they discovered about God they pass on to us, not as mere information but as an invitation to notice, to wonder, to question, and to realize for ourselves.

My purpose in spelling out these fundamental principles is to help sharpen what noticing means for the mind. In particular, my hope is that we will trust more profoundly our own capacity to notice, to question, and to uncover what is really going on in and around us. Our minds are not constructed any differently than the mind of any genius. Slower perhaps; more burdened with practical issues perhaps. But the greatest discoveries in science and, what is especially important for our purposes, the greatest discoveries about God began with people letting their curiosity be piqued by their experience—as much by inner experience as by what they see, hear, taste, smell, or touch.

## 2. WHAT TO NOTICE

Inner experience, however, is as massive, diverse, and subtle as what comes in through the five senses. Because of this we need to specify what particular areas to pay attention to in order to make a responsible decision about our lives.

Recall that when we respond to God's action in us, we share in the very life of God. We become God's continuing outer Word in history, impelled by God's continuing inner Word in our hearts. Our question about what to notice, then, becomes, What does God notice? In what part of human living is God most keenly interested in getting involved?

The answer has been spoken in the person of Jesus. He was perfectly obedient to the Spirit's promptings within, turning his head now this way, now that. We look to him as a model of how to pay attention.

An "Imitation of Christ" that goes beyond mere pious behavioral imitation does well to focus on how Jesus paid attention. Notice in particular the many things he did *not* pay attention to when his friends were trying to draw his attention—to the wonderful masonry in the temple, to the pressing needs in Martha's kitchen. Where was his heart at these moments? Although only by regular prayerful reflection on Scripture can we really grow familiar with the inner life of Jesus, let me offer a few general comments about what I see Jesus noticing.

First of all, Jesus noticed pain. He noticed it wherever he walked. The very sign of the Reign of God that he preached was that the blind see and the deaf hear. He had no "preferential option for the poor" when it came to pain. Rather, Jesus seemed to have a preferential option to cross all the human boundaries of social status, office, gender, age, and race in order to reach anyone who suffered in any way. He reached out to heal whoever he thought had faith enough to be healed. He noticed not only physical pain but emotional pain as well. He knew about comforting the sorrowful Martha and the agonizing Jairus. He noticed even the intellectual pain of Nicodemus and the pained faith of Thomas. He warned Peter that Satan would sift him like so much wheat.

Scripture does not describe Jesus' stream of consciousness, but the evidence is strong that he knew well the inner pain of his own heart. He may well have had physical and emotional pain as much as any of us, but he certainly suffered the pain of seeing his hopes collapse one after another. He suffered the pain of longing for the liberation of Jerusalem, wishing he could gather its people like a hen gathers her chicks. He even suffered the pain of not knowing why the Father forsook him at his most desperate hour.

To some degree these are pains we all experience, but we often repress the experience. We hide from the pain of others. We put off visiting a hospital or a funeral home. We do not even want to visit our own hearts. We avoid our own feelings of longing and loss. We smother our own hopes for our families, our schools, our governments. We ignore the feeling that God has abandoned us. Instead we run off into a darkness of frenzied activity and mindless talk.

People who suffer chronic pain are taught a paradoxical therapy: *Focus on the present pain.* Do not try to ignore it, but let yourself feel exactly what you are feeling at each present moment. But do not focus on either past or future pain. People who are afraid to allow present pain into consciousness will eventually feel their physical pain multiplied by an inner revolution of fear and anxiety over the thought that they have no resources for all the suffering that lies ahead. Only when present pain is acknowledged can our minds then deal with more practical matters at hand.

The same can be said even about the "pain" of being a responsible person with strong hopes and sturdy loves. It is indeed frightful to think about living the whole of life in what seems like one continuous struggle. Yet to ignore the pain of present affectivity, with the specter of heartbreak hovering over our hopes, tends to rob these hopes of the very power to achieve them.

In short, noticing pain is a path to noticing love. Every inner pain we experience, whether because we have noticed pain in others or because of some loss or obstacle in our own lives, is a signal that something we love dearly is threatened with death. It can come as a profound revelation when a person who has neglected pain in his or her life eventually faces it and discovers a deep but vulnerable desire. A retreat situation is an opportune time to allow our pains to surface. About each one we can ask the question, What is it that I love so much here?

The answer to this question can be frightful. On the one hand, not all love is a gift of God within us. When we swing open the cellar door of pain and let light shine down on a hidden love, we may discover a love that is consuming our best energies and draining us of genuine vitality. The beast must be tamed, even though it will plea-bargain to avoid the light.

On the other hand, there are often hidden treasures in that cellar, desires and loves that we were afraid to bring out into the light. Perhaps we feared that our families and friends would laugh at us. Or perhaps we feared we would have to sell everything we own in order to take full possession of that love. Yet when it is God loving in us, that love is a gentle, deep force that resonates with our whole souls. Yes, there are prices to pay and losses to incur when we let our best love take charge. But the Spirit of Love takes kindly even to its rivals. It does not demand that we slash and burn; it usually allows for a temporarily peaceful coexistence until our hearts, minds, and bodies make all the necessary adjustments for letting our truest love provide what we had hoped other loves would give us in times past.

The second thing Jesus noticed was joy. He noticed it preeminently in himself. We hear it when he rejoices that the Father has revealed the mysteries of the Kingdom to "mere children." We see it in John's version of Jesus' first miracle—delivering the finest wine to a wedding feast. Having an intimate experience of this kind of joy, Jesus longed for others to share in it. We can hear it in the Beatitudes, "Happy are you . . ." We hear it in his parables of the prodigal son, whose father was overjoyed, and of the women who found her lost coin. We see it in the Resurrection appearances as he wished his friends peace.

Still, Jesus knew that this kind of joy is not an easy experience to recognize, confused as it often is with mere pleasure or excitement. This is why he has to tell the crowds exactly what it is that makes them "happy." Part of the effect of the parables of the prodigal son, whose father is overjoyed, and of the women who found her lost coin was precisely to instruct others where this joy is to be found.

It is very important for a praxis of noticing to learn to recognize and savor this kind of joy. Jesus' joy is not simply about some general good fortune in the lives of people he cares for. It is specifically a joy that someone lost has been found, someone straying has returned, someone sour has joined a celebration. It is a joy that the Father has worked effectively in their lives, drawing them back into a loving relationship. Luke describes it in the infancy narratives as a joy that God is at work, lifting up the lowly to unexpected heights. It is a joy that rejoices that God would look with favor on oneself and speak a divine Word in one's own situation.

If I may venture an opinion having lived among faithful Christians all my life, I find that our chief temptation is to forget joy for the sake of "justice." Most of us are not powermongers or money grabbers. We struggle daily to keep a balance between too much and too little control over our lives. But our very fidelity can become that of the elder brother of the prodigal son. We forget how to drop the rake and come in to the party. This is the real terror of hell—that the gates are not locked! We are invited eternally by the Father to come to the celebration, but of our own choice we have grown to prefer a counterfeit fidelity that keeps accounts and measures, and so we labor on in a hell of self-righteousness, all the while resenting the noisy party going on in the house on the hill. "It is just not fair; it is just not fair; it is just not fair . . ."

No doubt there are other experiences besides pain and joy that Jesus noticed. And no doubt that what God notices can be found everywhere in the Old Testament as well as in what the disciples Paul, Luke, Philip, Stephen, and others noticed. The point is not to make a list of concepts but to learn the praxis of noticing what God notices. This requires both regular reflection on Scripture and a conscious effort to look at life around us with God's eyes.

"May the God of our Lord Jesus Christ, the Father of glory, give you a spirit of wisdom and perception of what is revealed, to bring you to full knowledge of him. *May he enlighten the eyes of your heart* so that you can see what hope his call holds for you, what rich glories he has promised the saints will inherit and how infinitely great is the power that he has exercised for us believers" (Eph 1:17–18).

## 3. NOTICING CONSOLATION AND DESOLATION

What I have called "consolation and desolation" are derived from Saint Ignatius' use of the terms. In chapter 2 I stressed the importance of learning from personal experience how to deal with these movements. Perhaps it is timely here to say something further about this special kind of interior noticing.

First, consolation and desolation are not two further experiences to add to the list of experiences of insight, verification, feelings, choices, wonder, and so on. Rather, they are the *affective context* of these inner experiences. For we do not simply experience inner movements apart from a dynamic orientation, a moral or religious horizon within which we are ruminating or plotting or dreaming. This is because all our conscious acts occur in the shadow of what we love.

What we love, however, may not be immediately evident. For example, we may feel heartsick over the deaths of two different neighbors. But upon examining our feelings of grief, we discover that in the case of the one neighbor we genuinely cared for the person, while in the case of the other we are losing no more than a generous carpenter or babysitter. It is our love that puts meaning into our noticing, understanding, realizing, feeling, and deciding.

Thus the basic question about our inner experiences becomes, What love is lifting these thoughts or feelings up within me? Ignatius considered that the *affective context* of our thoughts and feelings was far more important than their *objects*. In other words, before making any decision, while it is important to consider the costs and ramifications of various proposals, the ultimate personal question is whether or not we are moved by a love that God has given us.

It is no small achievement to grow accustomed to making the final criterion for choices one's love rather than the persons or projects one is considering. It means focusing more on the source of desire than its object. But the reason it is so important is that every choice we make is actually a double choice. We choose not only to do or say something; in the doing or saying, we are simultaneously choosing to be a self motivated by a certain kind of love. We are choosing to be in love in a very specific and concrete manner. People who neglect their love and use instead only external, ethical criteria for their choices often find that they cannot determine which alternative is "objectively better." They have forgotten that there is also an "objectively better" self involved in the choice as well.

Saint Ignatius inherited much wisdom on this subject but provided his own wisdom chiefly by subtraction. He seems to have pared down a great mass of medieval wisdom to a few rules so as to leave the individual to learn directly from experience as far as possible. I have paraphrased much of it in *Spiritual Exercises for Today* under "Dynamics of Spirit." For one thing, he realized that a person's moral horizon tends to maintain itself by affectivity and tends to change with rational thinking. In a person going from bad to worse, his feelings only reinforce the downward spiral into degenerate living while the rational sting of conscience tends to stop it. Conversely, a person going from good to better tends to trust her affections when making a decision but hesitates and becomes confused when too much rational analysis enters the picture.

Ignatius insisted that a person know the difference between consolation and desolation. Consolation is not always pleasurable nor is desolation always gloomy. It is consolation, for example, when a person sheds tears over his or her sins. And it is desolation when a person feels giddy and excited. Consolation is an experience of faith, charity, or hope; that is, consolation means appreciating something with God's eyes (faith), feeling empowered to loving someone with God's love (charity), or having confident desires about the future (hope). Desolation is the opposite of these. We find it difficult to appreciate much at all. Other people become just obstacles in our path. The future is forbidding.

Consolation can be either the joy or the pain we spoke of above. Above all we feel charged by love to go beyond our usual limits. It is a state not so much of higher energy as integrated energy, as all our inner resources seem governed by our love. It lifts us beyond the rational balance we try to maintain for the sake of objectivity and fills us with a quiet but courageous force.

Desolation, by contrast, tries to make excitement look like joy or pious melancholy look like loving sorrow. To put this in more contemporary terms, desolation is being "in a mood."[1] We see the world through colored glasses that filter out the full spectrum of values in everything we look at. The glasses may be "blue," rendering things and people sadder than they really are; or the glasses may be the familiar rose-colored that filter out dangers; or they may be an excitable yellow, a passionate red, or a stern gray. Usually there is something about the mood that we like, even though it fogs our moral vision.

The point of noticing consolation and desolation, of course, is to know when to make a choice that is free of compulsion and motivated by a love that originates in God. Thus, in desolation, it is unwise to make a decision, even though our reasoning may seem flawless. What is happening in desolation is that our value judgments are off; our heart is being choked by fear or ambition. Desolation is like a black hole in space, sucking in all nearby light by which we might appreciate what is truly good and disparage what is less good. We are temporarily blind both to the worth of actually taking a certain path and to the worth of ourselves as being a person filled with such and such a love.

It is important to recognize that when a friend or a fellow worker is "in a mood," he or she is not on the attack so much as under attack. If we feel another's mood as an intrusion on our own psyches and leap to the defense, we start a secondary war that diverts valuable attention away from the primary one.

To respond well to another's desolation, it is important first to determine why they are in the mood they are. If a good person is beaten down with too many thoughts, it does no good to add more rational considerations, helpful though they may be in another context. On the other hand, if the person's mood sprung from some affective negligence on their part, particularly from neglect of prayer or from mere self-indulgence, a good pinch in the right spot might wake them up to reality. In either case, I believe Ignatius once advised, "Treat others as their good spirit treats them"—in the first case with affection, assurance, patience, presence, and care; in the second with assertions, facts, information, considerations, and directives.

It is particularly unwise in desolation to pass judgment on our own behavior. True, we are not morally perfect. We go too far in our eating, drinking, buying, and stretching the truth to our own advantage. But the real damage comes when we indict ourselves for misdeeds far more vindictively than any of our friends—or God—ever would. I dare say that those guilt feelings which are accompanied by anxiety, worry, hesitation, and fear can never be trusted. Even though we have no doubt that we sinned, the true moral weight of the sin and the true worth of ourselves lies beyond our ken when in desolation. If we give in to the thoughts and feelings that come with desolation, we feel too ashamed to act in genuine love, we resent people who seem better than we are, and we lose heart about the future. The result, of course, is that we are rendered all the more prone to a further moral failure, giving us yet more evidence of our worthlessness and fruitlessness.

One of the worst effects of desolation is that it destroys our memory of consolation. We find it impossible even to imagine what it was like to be carried along in God's love for the world. Even if we acknowledge that we had experienced consolation at some time, we belittle its power and seriously doubt whether such a spiritual energizing is even possible for us in the future. Think of the times when you have loved wallowing in a mood—either high or low—and you will understand how prepossessing desolation can become.

In consolation, on the other hand, we experience a liberation of our value judgments. We find ourselves able to assess the worth of things even if attaining them will cost us pain. We easily reach out to others, appreciating their goodness. In consolation we do not need much effort to notice the pain and the joy in the world around us. Our love sees it clearly.

We can see even our own guilt well in consolation. It feels like a simple recognition of a truth in the presence of someone lovingly forgiving us. It was consolation when the prodigal son decided to return to his father, even though he felt constrained to accept a lowly place on the farm. It was certainly consolation when he felt his father's arms around him, even though at that moment he saw that his sin was worse than he had realized: he had not reckoned on the depths of the father's love against which he had sinned.

But—and this is an important "but"—while it is true that desolation can never be trusted, it is not true that consolation can always be trusted. Here is where the praxis of noticing must be exercised. As Ignatius describes it, the Evil Spirit can give consolation, can use not only the truth but the glow of peaceful conviction, in order to lead us to something worthless—or at least less worthy than some proposal we had entertained earlier. We make our mistakes because before we learn through experience the specific traps that we tend to fall into, we must experience falling into them.

In consolation therefore, it is very important that we notice not only the quality of the ideas and inspirations that strike us but even the quality of our assessment of our performance after the fact. In other words, we ought to examine our consciousness not only about upcoming events but also about situations we have recently experienced. The overriding question is, Was it your love, God, that moved me?

Let me suggest two major clues that point to a consolation that is not from God. The first is *self-image*. Often we think of some occupation, or of saying something to someone, that rushes upon us full of promise. We are excited about exploring the possibilities. But as we consider it, our hope is focused more on our own role, what it would feel like to do or say this, than on the effects of our choice in the world and on the people around us. We are focused not on the Reign of God but on our own advantage, even though there seems to be no harm to anyone.

Yet there is great harm in acting on self-love. The harm lies in overlooking the larger context of the Reign of God in everything that we do and, by omission, failing to meet the actual needs of our situation. The real sin of self-love, in other words, lies in a failure to love intelligently enough. It is basically a sin of omission, even though we decided to say or do something positive. In God's providence we were given at this moment both the love and the wits to see a much more worthwhile path, but we were busy trying to look good. It can become an insidious habit for those who need to look like God's ministers.

The other major clue to a consolation that we ought to hold suspect is the phenomenon of *closed access*. By closed access I mean any decision that effectively puts a block between people and their available resources. These resources may be the very basic needs for survival—clean water, shelter, clothes, nourishing food. They may be the material resources of a school or company—workplace, instruction books, copiers, paper, parking space, postage. They may be the resources of other people—for which we need access to offices, places to talk together, long distance phone calls, transportation.

This is a more difficult area to notice because we are
not accustomed to putting the question to ourselves. We
know that the answer will often take research and analysis
to determine who benefits and who suffers from our decisions. More important, it takes a praxis of social consciousness that regularly thinks of the benefits and costs to other
groups as well as our own. We are not only selfish as individuals, we are selfish as communities. But where the
community can often heal the individual egoist through affection, that same affection can often harden the community's heart to other communities. Communities will forever
wage turf wars, or at least as long as community or nation
or family commands a higher allegiance than obedience to
God's Spirit in our hearts and God's Word in our history.

Recognizing these cautions about consolation does not
mean hesitating before every decision, although hesitation
shapes history just as much as action does. We cannot test
a road without traveling it. So we have to trust the affectivity that we have and generally be prone to act on whatever
inspirations we experience.

Yet we can look back on the road we chose to see if the
decision was God's work in us. A very natural way of doing
this is to remember gratitude. At the end of each day we
can bring the good things we did or said to the Lord and
give heartfelt thanks. The efforts we initially thought were
good but turned out wrong will stand out because gratitude
will not come very easily. Then we can ask whether or not
a false consolation drew us away from something that was
actually better. The answers do not come easily, of course,
but over time the habit of thanking God for the graces of
the day will bring into relief the ungraced movements that
we tend to experience.

Thus noticing has two phases. We need to notice as
much as we can about a situation before moving to any decision—and this includes noticing the events of our hearts.
Then, after a decision, as we put our resolve into effect, we
should also pay attention to the concrete experience of mak-

ing our choice effective. There are often new clues, particularly within our hearts, that can lead us to reconsider the choice we made.

Between these two phases there is a great deal more that goes on. There is also the praxis of meditation, in which we aim to understand what we have noticed.

# CHAPTER SIX

---

# The Praxis of Meditation

*Meditation* is a common enough word in the spiritual life. In one sense we all know what it means. It refers to thinking about God and about our lives in a discursive, conceptual, analytical fashion. It has been contrasted with *contemplation*, which is a more restful, nondiscursive, nonanalytical focus on God and on ourselves in relation to God.

Yet from apostolic times up to the very present, the actual practice of meditation has narrowed the vision of the Reign of God presented in the New Testament and has stifled the creativity of Christians. Let me explain how this has happened and how a new understanding of the praxis of meditation is necessary for bringing about God's Dream in today's world.

## 1. THE HISTORY OF MEDITATION

From the beginnings of our race women and men have always wondered about why things happen and how to respond to them. And although we can point to thousands of practical insights reached by this or that culture, there gradually emerged the larger questions of the meaning of life, the essentials upon which history rides, and the wisdom whereby one could lead "the good life." Socrates is reputed to have been the first person who asked for a definition, and there the Greek philosophical tradition was born. Aristotle made the distinction between practical wisdom and theoretical wisdom and, in the realm of theoretical wisdom, established a basic set of terms with which to explain reality—"substance," "accidents," "nature," and so on.

In both the Platonic and Aristotelian strands of Greek "meditation," while there was a keen sense of the enduring mystery of life, there was also an expectation that the human mind could penetrate the mystery to some extent; in fact, the ideal of knowledge lay in grasping the unchanging essences of things in a way that lifted them above the history-bound aspects of life.

The Hebrew tradition of "meditation" took history far more seriously. From its beginnings Israel knew itself to be a historical community with a future different from its past, since it was being guided by the power of Yahweh, under legal covenant, to become a settled and respected nation. Israel meditated on the "Word of God," primarily as that Word shaped its history.[1] The significance of that Word lay in the *work* it accomplished, and only subsequently did "God's Word" refer to the texts that codified and chronicled that activity of God among them.[2] So there grew a body of legal and sapiential literature and the practice of meditating on that literature to see what meanings the past work of Yahweh held for the present time.

With the appearance of Mark's Gospel, a new literary form was created, a form quickly copied by the other Evangelists. The "gospel" was news that God had performed yet another work in contemporary times, which an "announcer" (evangelist) proclaimed through a narrative of the life, death, and raising up of a person. The Gospels themselves, then, were the product of Christian disciples "meditating" on something that recently occurred, either to themselves or to witnesses with whom they talked. Although the meaning and language of these occurrences were drawn from a range of relatively old texts in which God had promised to act in history or in which the person of Jesus was seen as prefigured, the focus of any meditation on these texts was to find meaning in present historical experience.³

During the next several centuries the great founding theologians of the church—Tertullian, Clement, Origen, Irenaeus, Athanasius, Gregory of Nyssa, Augustine, and others—continued to draw out the meanings not only from the Old Testament but now from the New. They pursued these meanings not only as creedal truths to believe but, as the monks and hermits of the age did, as intelligible "food for the soul."⁴ In letters, homilies, prayers, and both defensive and conciliatory treatises, they recorded the fruits of their meditations on the events described in the Bible, books that helped the ordinary Christian understand the Gospels and that set an example of the practice of meditation itself.

But at the same time, these theologians were constrained to defend the gospel in a Greek milieu, where the eternal aspects of God's Word had to be stressed. Because of this, although the Christian tradition challenged a variety of paganisms and gnosticisms by its belief in the historical work of God in the gift of Son and Spirit, it neglected to continue the style of meditation that sought to discern God's historical action in the postapostolic era.

Monasticism also contributed to dehistoricizing the Word by its ideal of an otherworldly union with God. By the fourth century, since the persecution of Christians had come to an end, the ideal of martyrdom had been replaced by the ideal of the monk, whose solitude was dedicated to reaching a union with God by meditating on texts. In Athanasius' *Life of Antony* (ca. 360) we read, "When finally the persecution ended, . . . Antony departed and withdrew once again to his cell and was there daily being martyred by his conscience."⁵ Antony wrote that the monk could receive God's mercy by "many studies of the word of God."⁶ Thus, radical Christianity became less missionary and more solitary, less prophetic and more ascetical, less conscious of the work of God around the Mediterranean basin and more interested in gaining ascetical wisdom from books, less aware of God's present work as Spirit and more of God's past work as Son. The Word of God was less a historical action and more a text to ruminate and digest as food for the soul.

Although the early desert hermits and celibates owed their faith to the Christ of the Gospels, they owed their style of living that faith not to any mainline biblical tradition (the Essenes may be an exception) but rather to Stoic / Neoplatonic philosophy and Indian asceticism. Where Plato and Plotinus provided the intellectual tradition of ascending to the real through contemplation, the Greek exposure to Indian Hinduism in the fourth century B.C.E. passed on the practical ideal of solitude and contemplation lasting, among the Greeks, into the second century C.E.

Not only did meditation become otherworldly, eventually the very practice of writing down meditations severed the direct connection between everyday life and Scripture. Meditation had become linked strictly with texts. The ideal was that spiritual reading should be followed by meditation, and meditation should be followed by either pious speaking or prayer. The texts meditated on were no longer strictly drawn from the Bible. By the eighth century monks had begun to produce books of prayerful reflection and of embellished biblical stories that gradually replaced the Bible and early Christian writings as the ordinary "book" of Christianity. These "meditations" were no doubt of some value, but insofar as they replaced rather than supplemented the more canonical literature, the historical sources that keep speculation tethered to reality were lost.

Furthermore, under the impetus of Bonaventure and the Franciscans of the twelfth century, books on *methods* of meditation began to appear. In spite of pervasive insistence that these methods were not to be followed rigidly, emphasis now shifted to technique, to fixed steps that presumably would lead to an understanding and relish of divine mysteries. But the "mysteries" in question, while they referred to the historical words and works of Jesus, did not refer to the continuing historical work of God in the late Middle Ages themselves. (It seems that the very centrality of Christ, in whom God inaugurated the Messianic Age, effectively prevented Christians from expecting any further historical epochs unfolded by the hand of God.) Again, there may be some value in technique for beginners, but insofar as technique replaced rather than supplemented the individual's wonder about his or her own situation, it lost the historical as well as the inner sources that tether speculation to reality.

Throughout this entire development of meditation styles, from Origen all the way to Vatican II, one ideal remained constant: the ideal of ascending to God in meditation, to the exclusion of furthering one's understanding of God's saving work in one's contemporary situation. As an imaginal theology of history, it was an interruptive vision, with dialectical aspects restricted to the spiritual lives of individuals. The writings of Hugh of St. Victor, Teresa of Avila, and John of the Cross reinforced an already overwhelming impression that union with God was a matter of "ascending" through stages of meditation, to contemplation, all in preparation for the beatific vision in the afterlife. We should not overlook, however, that Teresa and John were reformers as much as mystics, although in their writings they left no written meditations on their social and political labors for the Kingdom. We can learn from their performance that they also meditated on how to do God's will in their concrete situations.

It is easy to say now, after the nineteenth-century breakthroughs in historiography and the emergence of a progressive worldview, that historical consciousness was absent in the West, but it is important to understand the reasons for this. Aristotle's opinion that there could be no science of change was an intellectual swamp that only the daring would cross. The middleplatonisms of Clement and Origen and the Neoplatonism of Augustine reinforced an imaginal legacy of a world fallen from an original unity and in which we, as pilgrims or exiles, should raise our minds and hearts ever higher to God and things of heaven.[7]

This derailment of Christian meditation into technique and ahistorical conceptualism may seem incredible in face of the fact that the Bible has no such ideal of union with God through this ascensional meditation / contemplation. Rather, there is the powerful and sustained image of a God who acts in history, who desires first a faithful, covenanted community and then a Dynasty in which people are challenged: "to act justly, to love tenderly, and to walk humbly with your God."

The focus of New Testament meditation was not an unhistorical God but a history-making God. There is Mary, who "pondered these things in her heart"—"these things" meaning not texts but her own experience. There is Nicodemus, who is less concerned with rising up to heaven than with the alluring prospect of being "born again" on earth. There is Philip, who explains to the Ethiopian pilgrim reading Isaiah that the text refers to events that occurred not half a dozen years before. There is the repeated experiences of Peter and Paul, who see God continuing to work (credited at times to the Lord Jesus and at times to the Holy Spirit) in the present lives of believers.

I do not mean to suggest that monasticism and the desire for intimate union with God have no enduring value in themselves. Nor am I suggesting that the public life-style of Jesus is a divine condemnation of eremitic life. The problem lies in how these traditions emphasized starting with texts rather than with historical experience that texts might illuminate. The dynamic eschatology of Jesus, with its tension between history and eternity, had become replaced by a static Greco-Indian cosmology, where the tension is between the world above and the world below, or between spirit and body.[8] The Word of God had become sterilized into a literary object for Christian understanding and affection rather than a presently active force in history.

The beginnings of this shift can be discerned in the biblical texts themselves. If we read the New Testament in chronological order—from Paul's letters, through the syn-

optics, to the Johannine works—we see a growing emphasis
on the preexistence of Christ and on the nature of his person, along with a growing body of the very texts themselves
as vehicles of the gospel instead of the living word passed
from believer to believer. These further questions about the
life of Christ and his status before God were prompted as
much by a disciple's willingness to defend beliefs against
pagan skepticism as by a desire to understand the God one
loves.

The problem with defensive writing, however, is that it
is the opponent who frames the question and fixes the language, leaving even successful defenders speaking a borrowed tongue. The notion of God's "providence," for example,
is a term brought home from battles with the Stoics; to this
day, Christians have trouble defending it in the face of world
wars and the suffering of the innocent.

Eventually Christ was proclaimed as "God from God"
in a way that recognized his divine status. But this great
achievement in clarifying the truth about Jesus was understood and imagined in the Neoplatonic mode of a celestial
unity spilling down a descending ladder of diversity, forget-
ful of the raw, direct experience of mystery in the flesh to
which the first disciples gave witness. How different Christianity would be today if instead of understanding Jesus and
the Spirit in the ahistorical categories already used by
Greeks about God, they came to understand God in the
history-laden categories already used by Jews about Jesus
and the Spirit![9]

It could also be argued, I believe, that from the very
beginning the principles of authority implicit in the good
news have been overshadowed by the way authority was actually exercised among Jews and Greeks at the time. I am
thinking not only of such texts as "I have come to serve, not
to be served" but of the equality-in-tension of God's Word
and God's Spirit. It is the recurring problem of how to balance inspiration at the local level with the need for a cen-
tralized authority. Paul dealt with the problem in two ways.

First, he taught his doctrine of one Spirit and many gifts, all of which should lead to the same end. But, if his extant letters are any indication, he also decided to refer to the Spirit less and less frequently, diminishing steadily to zero in the letter to the Colossians.[10]

The issue here is power. The perennial temptation of Christian authorities is to hold the center at the expense of the periphery. Much safer to have a monarchical, Neoplatonic God, along with a necessarily hierarchical framework for earthly authority, than the more subtle trinitarian God who, in Jesus, is forever skeptical of those who lord it over others and, in the Spirit, chronically shatters the expectations of the most pious believers.[11] Had Christian meditation of the significance of experience stood its ground in the tradition, perhaps the Holy Spirit would be "worshiped and glorified" indeed.

## 2. THE NEW QUESTIONS

This sad history leaves us with a choice. Shall we dump the terms *meditation* and *contemplation,* with all their overtones of shirking responsibility for the world and leaving responsibility strictly to those in charge or shall we keep them in the hope of giving them new meaning? Obviously, I believe we should keep them.

I believe so not only because of their revered pedigree but because the otherworldly overtones were due not to the acts of meditation and contemplation themselves but to the unhistorical objects of these acts. Our minds are still capable of analytical, discursive reasoning (meditation) as well as an affective, nonconceptual appreciation (contemplation), even though we need not restrict our meditation to individual virtues and the eternal goodness of God.

How then shall we meditate today? The answer depends on a prior choice about *whose questions are most relevant for us.* This is true whether or not we notice it. Most of our questions about God, life, death, and love are inherited from a community with a specific perspective and set of concerns; few if any arise exclusively from our own experience. Jesus surely meditated on the questions felt by the poor in spirit, the gentle, those who mourn, those who hunger and thirst for justice, the merciful, the pure of heart, peacemakers, and the persecuted—not because of his personal experience alone but because he understood the bewilderments of people whose lives were hemmed in by legal proscriptions and the caprice of the powerful.

Today, the Second Vatican Council of the Roman Catholic Church has directed our attention to "the joys and the hopes, the griefs and the anxieties of the people of this age, especially those who are poor or in any way afflicted."[12] I have already mentioned how both pain and joy are among the most important things to notice in life. This is true of any age, of course. Whether or not we choose to, we will meditate on the questions of those whose joys and pains we share. The breadth of our meditation, therefore, will depend on the breadth of our noticing. And the breadth of our noticing depends on exposure to the lives of people unlike ourselves. To welcome the stranger is more than a corporal work of mercy; it is, as Jesus taught, a welcome of God's perfect Word. So the first precept we can formulate on how to meditate today is: Notice joy and pain beyond your own fence.

We saw that noticing generates questions. But our culture has inherited new kinds of questions not to be found in either the Bible or in the greater part of Christian tradition. These new questions can give direction to what we meditate on and how our meditation should proceed. Let me name three areas where fundamental questions have been posed, questions unheard of in the Middle Ages or before, questions whose answers are still unfolding in our own time.

1. *How to read the Bible.* The science of hermeneutics and the various critical methods used by Scripture scholars have pulled the rug out from under the settled view that the

words in the Bible are clear and unambiguous. We cannot simply use scriptural texts for meditation without understanding how their authors intended these texts to be read. It helps meditation greatly not only to have accurate translations but also accurate commentaries that introduce the new reader to the often baffling mindsets of the scriptural authors, who, after all, remain cultural foreigners.

Yet after retrieving what the authors meant by their texts and being aware that their audiences really had the final say about which texts represented orthodox Christian meanings, today's reader should know how to let the texts still have their powerful effect. We therefore face the question whether it is legitimate to read the texts not only as historical good news but as metaphors for our present experiences. We also struggle to determine which aspects of Jesus' words and deeds—particularly today about authority in the church—cannot be modified by history and which can. It takes loving meditation to draw meaning from Scripture that is legitimate for today.

2. *How to regard historical progress.* Since the Enlightenment and up to the vision of Karl Marx, the Western mind has energetically regarded history as something over which humans ought to have control. Two world wars and the mass murders of Hitler and Stalin and the Chinese Revolution notwithstanding, science and economics have enthusiastically tried to direct the course of history as far as possible. The preservative and interruptive images of history have yielded the place of honor to a progressive vision that still expects to find ways to improve the standard of living, to overcome diseases, to settle international disputes, and to hold the reins on a global economy.

The progressive mindset will either laugh Christian pietism off the stage or will challenge Christians to acknowledge the progress of humanity and to create ways to direct it along lines consistent with Christian values. This requires not merely a Christian concern for social justice

but a theological understanding of how God is personally
and actively present in history as both Son and Spirit. It
means meditating on God as one who not only has mercy on
sinners but who fills us with a spirit of creative and shrewd
love for neighbor.

3. *How to validate Christian action.* Up to the recent past,
and for many Christians even today, the most religiously
relevant action in a Christian's life took place at rituals—
especially baptism, Sunday Eucharist, weddings, the rite of
reconciliation, and the anointing of the sick. The extension
of these rituals into daily life was chiefly a matter of avoid-
ing sin, forgiving offenses, being faithful to prayer, and setting a good example. It seemed enough simply to perform
these actions, without paying much attention to their effectiveness in propagating the Kingdom.[13] Their justification
was simply the injunctions of church leaders who, at best,
appealed to similar injunctions in Scripture and the tradition. Essentially Christian action was validated by authority rather than by any insight into its effectiveness in
turning people's hearts of stone into hearts of flesh.

But with the revolution in empirical science, men and
women test the validity of any enterprise by looking to results rather than authorities. No doubt there is a problem
of how to measure results that lie in unquantifiable values
and meanings, but blind obedience to the voice of authority
does not even merit the adjective *intelligent* in an adult.
Thus, we increasingly find that Christians wonder about
policies and ethical pronouncements of both politicians and
church authorities. Few doubt the right of authorities to
have their say, but many will give only partial assent to
official policies that they know from experience will not
speak to the people close to them. Here meditation will be
the living bridge between law, discipline, and tradition on
the one hand and actual human agonies, needs, and hopes
on the other.

Validation by effectiveness is not a new ideal stemming from modern scientific method. In the Acts of the Apostles and the letters of Paul, we see frequent changes in apostolic strategies and language for the sake of making the good news hit home. To the Jews at Antioch Paul preaches the good news as a fulfillment of a promise. To believers in Zeus and Hermes it is the fulfillment of a "natural theology." To Epicurean and Stoic philosophers it becomes a revelation of an "unknown god" whom they already worship. Or recall Peter's worrying over his vision of the sheetful of animals and his eventual realization that God has called the Gentiles as well as Jews. Clearly these profound shifts in attitude resulted from an intelligent concern that the good news of Christ Jesus reach people in a language they understand.[14]

These are at least some of the new questions that define the present world—a world God longs and labors to save. It will not be easy to work out answers to them. But as colaborers with God we ought to take these questions to heart ourselves, even if it means reconceiving the praxis of meditation.

The new style of meditation will have several features.

1. It will be aware of the problems of interpreting scriptural texts and yet be intent on using these texts to encounter the mystery of God's self-gift to humanity.

2. It will use not only common sense but also the tools of social, economic, and psychological analysis of situations.

3. It will meditate not merely to understand the present and the past but to create intelligent strategies, with feedback, to undo evil and bring reconciliation where it can.

4. It will meditate within a conscious knowledge that the meditation itself is not a ladder to reach God but God's own work in the soul to bring about the Kingdom through our own healing and creative powers.

5. It will love the world with God's love but without loss of the biblical ideal where God is loved with one's "whole heart, whole soul, whole mind, whole strength."

## 3. MEDITATION AS UNDERSTANDING THE CONCRETE MEANING OF LOVE

Our aim, you will recall, is to create a grammar of retreat by a language that connects spiritual events to acts of consciousness. "Praxis" is not technique; nor is it simply the ability to meditate, contemplate, imagine, discern. Rather, it is the ability to perform these spiritual actions knowingly, with growing understanding of how they function in the spiritual life, how they relate to one another, what their specific limits are, what their effects might be on history, and how to talk about them with others.

In this section I would like to give meditation a definition that may help readers locate the event in themselves and to see, through personal inner experience, how it is connected to other inner events.

> *Meditation is understanding the concrete*
> *meaning of love.*

Let us look at the major terms in this definition:

*Meaning.* To notice in ourselves the kind of meditation found in Scripture we need only recall the recurring question, What does it all mean? We ask that question about many things in life. It is not a question about what we should do. Nor is it a question about what the long-range implications of some experience may be. It is first of all a question of the meaning of an experience.

But what is *meaning?* Because we use the word in several different senses, perhaps a few examples will help to clarify the breadth of the word. Recently I read in a newspaper column a reader's question, "How do you explain the difference between 'hypothetical' and 'theoretical'? My dic-

tionary doesn't do it at all well." There the reader was looking for the meaning of a word in a dictionary. But diction-
aries often fail to satisfy our curiosity because the meaning
of a word depends on *who* means it. In other words, we have
to pay attention to the concrete, particular act of meaning
in a person as well as to the abstract, common definition of
the word.

Another example: A Vietnam war veteran may ask,
"What did the war mean?" But very soon the answer focuses
on *who* meant to wage the war, for what purposes, and so on.

Finally, the broadest example: From time to time everyone asks, "What does it all mean?" We ask this about life,
death, and love. We ask it about the mismatch between lofty
human ideals and miserable human malice. But here too
the meaning of "life" leads to the question of a *who* that
means it.

That *who* is ourselves, certainly, and our forebears, but
it is also the one we call God. Even atheists experience the
question of life's meaning in this sense. But to meditate on
the meaning of life—whether life in general or some specific
life experience—is to meditate on *what people and God intend* by their words and deeds. This is the object of a meditation, the reality we meditate on. To meditate about love's
meaning, therefore, is to wonder about not only the various
cause-effect connections we see but especially about the purposes, the intentions, the desires of the agents involved.

*Understanding.* But what about the act of meditation
itself? It has been called "discursive thinking," but what
exactly is that? Let us use the familiar word *understanding*
to refer to the act by which we grasp meaning.

By understand I mean that meditation seeks to answer
why or how. It aims to see connections, to get the insight, to
grasp the inner coherence of events. Its immediate purpose
is not to feel more deeply or to praise anyone or to be contrite or to give assent to what it already understands. These
may follow upon a fruitful meditation, but the key element

in meditation itself is the act of understanding, which is the source of our concepts, our explanations, and of the meanings we test for truth and worth.

To learn the praxis of meditation means being able to know when we understand and when we do not. Often we are too ready simply to appear intelligent, too proud to admit we did not understand this or that paragraph in a book, or too shy to say "I don't get it." Sometimes we substitute facts we have memorized in place of understanding the historical realities that give these facts meaning. Or we substitute clever ways to talk about things instead of insight into the things we are talking about. "Women forgive but don't forget; men forget to forgive." Neat, but is it true? Or we simply pretend that we have mastered some subject— "Oh, yes, I read Jones's book on that."

The real damage in this intellectual dishonesty is that we lose familiarity with the act of insight itself. If we hide our lack of understanding from others, we eventually hide it from ourselves, so that we actually believe we understand, and we put aside any further questions because we no longer remember distinctly the experience of wondering why and then understanding why.

The praxis of meditation is not content with mere understanding. It also wants to test that understanding to see if it is correct. Ideas are easy to come by; what counts is verifying, testing, validating those ideas in the concrete. We do this through the act of judgment. This function of judgment returns to the data that the understanding seeks to explain and, as I pointed out in "The Praxis of Noticing," poses any further questions that pop up. In other words, meditation is more than an exercise in fancy. It seeks to understand what God and people really mean, and it intends to improve life in the concrete future. It has reality as its goal.

When we understand anything—the behavior of a friend, the implications of a choice to quit one's job, the meaning of Jesus' words "the Kingdom may be compared to a mustard seed"—it is not merely friends or jobs or words that we understand. We understand the relationships between things. We see the connection between a friend's behavior and a recently received letter; we envision the ramifications of quitting our job; we discern an analogy between the mustard seed and our own faith.

If a retreat aims to assess and integrate *relationships,* meditation provides the prior understanding that we need to assess the worth of any relationship. It is a necessary step in making a good choice.

*Love.* Finally, the relationships in question are about what we love. This is not a moral precept implying that we should meditate only on what we love. It is a truism. "Where your treasure is, there your heart will be." What we love always governs what we think about. True, since none of us loves well, we feel an obligation to turn our attention away from unworthy objects of love. We experience the need to meditate in order to understand explicitly the God, the world, the neighbor, and the self that we love. But we do not always follow that need. "He who closes his eyes meditates mischief; she who purses her lips has already done wrong" (Prv 16:30). This too is meditation.

As you can see, this rather empirical definition suggests that we meditate all the time, but not always within the framework of God's love. It is important to recognize this so as to become familiar with our own actual practice of meditating. In particular, recognizing that we meditate clarifies the real issue: For love of what (or whom) am I meditating?

But even those who love God can get so lost in the labyrinth of meditation that they forget the love that drew them to meditation in the first place. I have found that when the understanding becomes overloaded with ill-fitting insights, it helps greatly to stop the analysis and simply recall, with affection, the people whose relationships mean so much to me. So the meditation is not paying off today; at least do not leave it without a few moments of loving welcome of this encounter with mystery. Often this return to the full real-

ity—to our own felt relationship to what we want to understand—eliminates peripheral questions and highlights the
important ones.

Beginning and ending a meditation by tapping the love
that seeks understanding is particularly helpful in trying
to understand our relationship to ourselves. The very power
of our intellects to understand can suggest to us that there
is no ultimate mystery about ourselves, that there is available some ultimate rational control over our lives. And when
that intellect fails, we drop into worry like a stone down a
well.

But we are indeed a mystery. We always will be. It is
the very mystery of ourselves that others love in us. When
a friend says, "Take care of yourself," the meaning is "Take
the kind of care of yourself that I would like to be able to
do, for I love the mystery of who you are." Taking that kind
of care does not mean "understand yourself," nor does it
mean "pamper yourself." It means "honor the mystery of
who you are." Here, where understanding fails, is where
meditation becomes contemplation. But more about this in
the next chapter.

## 4. THE PURPOSE OF MEDITATION

People may meditate either for lofty or degrading purposes. But God's purpose in giving us intellects is to *love
intelligently*.

What or whom are we to love intelligently? Jesus told
us explicitly: "Listen, Israel, the Lord our God is the one
Lord, and you must love the Lord your God with all your
heart, with all your soul, with all your mind and with all
your strength. The second is this: You must love your neighbor as yourself" (Mk 12:30). Without this purpose in mind,
without this desire in our hearts, the practice of meditation
can close in upon itself and settle for the intellectual con-
solations of understanding a few things about the world we
live in.

In practice, intelligence serves love in two ways. It clarifies what a situation actually is, and it envisions what it could actually become—that is, it gathers the past and moves to the future. You will recall that we have defined a retreat as any withdrawal from immediate concerns to assess and integrate our relationships. The assessment phase clarifies and evaluates the situation; the integration phase alters existing relationships as we move into the future by our choice.

*Assessing the present.* In the first way, meditation serves the ascensional phase of a retreat by understanding the present situation. This means getting insights into one's life, grasping what is going on or what people mean by their words, and verifying these insights to see if they make sense of experience.

Assessment in a retreat means understanding our social roles, what others expect of us and what we expect from ourselves. It means wondering why people behave as they do. It means finding more vitality in questions about the human drama than in answers. It is in this mode that we get insight into our own operative ideals: "I don't make waves"; "I never let people down"; "I feel I ought to be a better parent." It has the power to unmask the myths thrust on us from either our own subconscious or our culture.

Yet all these psychological, sociological, and historical insights occur within a person's prior understanding of God and history—transcendence and time—which we discussed in chapters 3 and 4. It is important, therefore, not to lose sight of the fact that God is a real agent in one's psychology, community, and history, particularly inasmuch as current psychology, sociology, and historiography regard God at best as a belief system and not a reality.

Therefore this first way of meditation also means understanding various passages in Scripture, getting insight into Christ's words and his work, into the role of a disciple, into the nature of the early Christian churches, into the variety of ways the good news was preached. It also means being able to admit that we do not understand a certain passage in Scripture. It means recognizing that certain prayers in the liturgy have no meaning for us.

The examination of conscience functions partly within this mode of meditation. There we try to understand not only what we are feeling and thinking but out of what spirit as well. We try to see the connections between spiritual consolation or desolation on the one hand and the thoughts that strike us and the activities we engage in on the other.

*Integration for the future.* Meditation serves love in a second way by envisioning change. This means planning, policy-making, and strategizing. It means creatively using the procedures and ideal types of psychology, sociology, political science, and economics to make one's choice broadly effective.

More basically, however, we cannot move to the future without exploring the meaning of our own conversion. Before strategizing it is necessary to realize what God means and what we now mean, now that we have been touched by God's Word and Spirit.

To do that well meditation envisions life from an integral perspective. It sees our own religious experience as part of the larger process of God's Kingdom coming. Then we can more easily foresee what the Reign of God might be in this day. Our conversion usually gives us an intimate understanding of the particular dynamic of sin that characterizes the present age and grasps how it might best be turned around.

Then, from our inner experience and from our experience of "the joys and the hopes, the griefs and the anxieties" of our brothers and sisters, from reading, discussion, and reflection, we learn just how the perennial tension between grace and malice is felt in hearts today and how it might best be addressed. We can then "meditate" on more practical issues such as military armaments or the homeless with a view to helping God accomplish something of the Kingdom in the foreseeable future.

The examination of conscience also plays a role in integrating our relationships after a choice has been made. You will recall from chapter 5 on the praxis of noticing that we can try to do good under the inspiration of a bad spirit. This happens when some segment of our well-meant activity has been tainted by a mood or a compulsion we did not notice. There is a need to meditate on our reactions to our own activity to see if there are any hints of an incompletely integrated choice or a biased love at work.

Between meditating on how things stand and on how things might be, yet another important function is needed to bring about the Kingdom. No matter how clearly we understand the present situation, it is quite another matter altogether to evaluate the situation, to go beyond mere rational analysis to a moral judgment about the people that are worth listening to, about the worth of the social and economic arrangements that condition everyday life, about the quality of the mores, habits, and preferences of a community, and so on. In other words, between any kind of research phase and planning phase, there is a need for an ethical or moral phase that passes judgment on the past and takes a stand toward the future.[15]

For a Christian this means more than mere moral reflection, as important as that is. It means moral reflection under the conscious impulse of God's own love for the world. Notice that I am not saying that we Christians should rely merely on an inherited set of moral principles by which we measure life, although we do indeed have much to say to the world about the sanctity of the individual or the sanctity of local self-determination. Such moral principles are always interpreted and applied by real men and women, and their use of the principles will vary according to their familiarity with the love of God for the world as they have experienced it in their own hearts.

To be more precise, we should say that between meditating on how the land lies and meditating on which valleys should be filled and which mountains leveled, there is a need

for a love-inspired discrimination of values. It is a need to
get in touch with our love in a manner that, paradoxically,
does not want to improve things—at least not immediately.
It is the need to savor what is good in a situation and to be
sickened over what is rotten. It is the need simply to appreciate the beloved, without trying to fix what still remains
broken. It is the very human need to stand in awe over the
mystery of the other, whether that other is a spouse, a
friend, an entire family, a race, or our self-giving God. And
no less is it the incapacity to act when faced with the mystery of sin, hatred, and mutual destruction.

In other words, between these two ways of meditation
there is the need for contemplation. This contemplation will
not only relish values; it will also rest in reality, in the truth
one realizes. Again, as we anticipated in our Circle of
Praxis, there will be a place for this kind of contemplation
both before and after one makes a strategic choice about
one's life. At the same time, both modes of contemplation
are sandwiched between the two modes of meditation—not
necessarily in chronological sequence, but insofar as the
prechoice mode of meditation gives way to a contemplation
that rests a while in the divine reality and then as the
postchoice contemplation calls for meditation on the divine
consequences for God's Sovereignty over our history.

# CHAPTER SEVEN

---

# The Praxis of Contemplation

## 1. A MIXED LEGACY

Contemplation has carried so many different meanings in history that any attempt to define it would seem historically ignorant and dogmatically brash. Theological and philosophical encyclopedias presume often strikingly different definitions and so give inconsistent explanations of the same historical figures, be they mystics, reformers, or sages.

We can find two general trends, however. In the first the works of Plotinus and Augustine stress a contemplation that is the purpose of action and is the highest form of human living. In the second the works of Thomas Aquinas stress that on this earth contemplation finds its perfection in the action of teaching others and that contemplation in itself is not a mystical abstraction but ordinary, maturing human wisdom.[1]

Most writers agree at least (1) that the object of contemplation is either "God" or some transcendent object of our love; (2) that contemplation is a higher kind of knowing than meditation; and (3) that it is more "restful" than other kinds of knowing.[2]

But the agreement ends right there. Some think contemplation is rare, others common. Some make it a passive experience, others something active, others still a passive experience in the midst of action so that "contemplation in action" has become an ideal. Some want to distinguish a natural or acquired contemplation versus an infused contemplation, while others insist that in practice there is no way to tell the difference. Some include the various Old Testament theophanies and prophetic visions as contemplations, and others do not. Some think the otherworldly connotations of the term originate from Plato, Plotinus, Origen, and Augustine and not from Scripture, while others cite the Johannine writings to illustrate Christ in explicit contemplative union with the Father.

In Christian writings the notion of contemplation was not so much the victim of the ahistorical focus of "meditation" as it was the ideal toward which meditation was merely a step. Because of the Plotinian emphasis on the eternal and constant unity behind all things earthbound, *contemplation* became the word for the highest possible human knowledge of God—so high that a human could not achieve it unless God freely chose to give it. This drew a picture of a God that finished creating on the sixth day and was simply waiting for the sinful exiles finally to escape history in an afterlife, sparingly bequeathing glimpses of the divine essence to a chosen few.

These many interpretations of contemplation illustrate the general problem of giving names to any internal experience whatsoever. On the one hand, we need a word to direct our attention to the specific experiences we are talking about. On the other hand, we need to notice a certain sharply delimited set of experiences if we are to tag them with any word.

For example, the word *sad* used to mean "sober and content" but has gradually slid down the range of emotional experience and landed, for the present, at meaning "unhappy and discontent." Unlike sad, however, the meaning of contemplation slides around because so few people claim to have experienced it, and too many have tried to control its meaning by jamming it into categories drawn from a philosophy inimical to the kind of revelation that comes through the gospel.

You will recall that our project of creating a grammar of retreat draws its basic terms from events that occur in consciousness, events that are easily verifiable and intelligibly connected to other inner events. For example, we saw that "noticing" happens in everyone and that it links experience with some question or other. It happens more frequently and more fruitfully in the person who desires to live in the truth. Likewise, we saw that meditating is essentially an act of understanding but that it includes verification (by a return to what was noticed) and regards what or whom a person loves.

Before rushing to a similar definition of contemplation, let me explain the purpose and limits of such a definition. My purpose is to give not the final word but rather an initial definition that will need filling out by men and women with various experiences of contemplation. Still, I believe it is prudent to use *contemplation* to refer to a relatively ordinary, identifiable experience. I have the impression that many writers on mysticism, who because of a false humility never expect to experience an intimate knowledge of God, keep contemplation at a safe distance from themselves by overglorifying it in others.

Also, I feel that I am speaking directly to practitioners in the spiritual life, to people who not only live in the spirit but, because of their desire to help others intelligently, understand the need for words that explain, not merely describe. I am aware, however, that the historian of mysticism as well as the Sunday homilist would profit from the kind of definition I offer.

## 2. A DEFINITION

In the hermeneutic circle of giving names to experiences, what counts most are the experiences we want to notice. So let us begin by noticing what appears to be the most common experiential factors among those who already use the term *contemplation:*

1. The object of contemplation will be what we love. In particular, it will be the transcendent object of our love that lies both within and yet beyond the known persons and communities we love.

2. Contemplation is a higher form of knowing than meditation. Meditation leads to it and finds its fulfillment in it.

3. Contemplation has the quality of "resting." It does not ask questions and does not give explanations.

My definition runs thus:

> *Contemplation is realizing and appreciating the*
> *concrete meaning of love.*

By this definition I am opting to include certain disputed features of the term and ruling out others. Contemplation will be common, not rare. It will be passive in the sense that it does not entertain questions but active in that it welcomes, appreciates, values, or savors what we love. It does not always reveal whether its source is love for God or not, since just as evildoers can meditate mischief, so hedonists can contemplate what they love. It definitely would include the theophanic and prophetic experiences of the Old Testament considered essentially as inner events rather than mere fireworks in nature. And its meaning derives not from descriptions of philosophers or theologians but from our own noticing, understanding, and verifying that we do realize and appreciate what our love means in the concrete.

Finally, because this definition points toward the concrete meaning of love, without predetermining what that meaning must be, it is easily identified with the experiences recorded in the New Testament, not only of the disciples but particularly of Jesus himself. At the same time, it is also easily identified with experiences of people of any or no religion, thus giving us a basis for dialog among world religions or philosophies.

Let us look more closely at the elements of the definition. Again, I invite you to notice in yourself the events to which the definition refers.

*The concrete meaning of love.* We saw in the last chapter that love is the meaning of anything and everything. The question, What does it all mean? is also, at its root, the question, Who is this who means it? We experience our hearts being drawn toward something or someone beyond any earthly person or community we know. We normally feel this draw through the simple experiences of wishing others well, of wanting to do a good job, of dressing and walking with dignity, and of the many other ways we experience benevolence about life. But while we feel the draw constantly, we usually are so focused on the people and projects toward which we are drawn that we do not notice the draw itself.

Yet there are times when we are keenly aware of this pull on our attention. We focus not on practicalities or abstractions but on this recurring desire just as we experience it. We make room for it in consciousness by driving out thoughts about what we should do or what we should say. Then the mystery that dwells underneath ordinary things comes to life. These are times when what we gather through the five senses or what we experience welling up in our hearts appears to be a massive and simple word of love being spoken, as if creation itself was trying to assure us that we are well cared for.

Whether or not we follow this pull on our consciousness, whether or not we call its origin and object God, we all experience this transcendent movement. Even though we cannot lay eyes on the Beyond that draws us, we can still recognize and welcome the effects of that magnetism on our souls. We can notice it in our delight over a sunrise or in our response to the innocent faces of children. In a reverse way we can realize how this transcendent dimension of life seems to be missing when we ache for victims of an earthquake we have seen on television or when we agonize at the bed of a friend suffering a painful disease.

By the "concrete meaning of love," then, I am referring simultaneously to what we love and to the experience of loving. I am harking back to what we discovered in chapter 3—that the question of God is a double question, to which God gives a double reply through the outer Word for us to love and an inner Word with which to love. Often one of the biggest blocks to the praxis of contemplation is a too-fixed gaze on the object of our thoughts. Then it is time to relax and allow the experiences of desire, wonder, and love to work on their own, as it were. The experience of being drawn is as vital to contemplation as the Beyond that beckons us.

What we are contemplating is not simply what we know, however. We contemplate the mystery that both what we love and our experience of loving did not have to be. They are both there in a way beyond our control. We did not invent them. We even resist their visitations on our consciousness. Yet life and love close in on us and demand contemplative attention.

This too is concrete in the sense that our experience can point to data at a given time and place. We may not understand this transcendent thirst we feel, and we may find it difficult to talk about, but it is nonetheless a real force inviting us to savor and avow the mystery in everyday life.

*Realize and appreciate*. These are key words in the spiritual life. I will discuss them in more detail below. Briefly put, to realize something is to make a judgment of fact—this is true; this is so; I must acknowledge it. To appreciate something is to make a judgment of value—this is good; this is worthwhile; I cannot help but honor it.

Notice especially what realizing and appreciating are not.

1. They are not insights—that is, they do not yield understanding. By themselves they do not enable us to give an

explanation to anyone. It is meditation that gives us insight. Indeed, contemplatives are often speechless.

2. They are not emotions, although emotions may accompany them. In particular, emotions usually precede a judgment of value, but we can remain convinced of the value of something and make hard choices based on our evaluation long after our feelings about it have abandoned us.

3. They are not mental images. Sometimes contemplatives use imagination to open the mind and heart, but once they realize and appreciate something, they go beyond imagination to claim an objective truth and an objective value. When constrained to speak to others about their contemplative experience, they may use images, but only as a means to draw others into a similar realization and appreciation about the full meaning of their own love.

These first three items are particularly important to remember during those days when our spiritual energies pull in opposite directions. When we experience spiritual desolation, our understanding, feelings, and imagination can either die on us or run amok. In any case, they do not pull together harmoniously in a way that helps our love. But while it is difficult to feel in love at times like this, the truth is that we *are* in love, whether or not we understand it, feel it, or imagine it. We can still affirm the truth. So contemplation can go on even in this winter of the psyche. In fact, there are certain realizations—particularly about the real limits of our own abilities—that come only when we contemplate some actual love during desolation. Likewise, it is surprising how easily we can appreciate the burdens of others when our small load has bent us double.

4. Realizing and appreciating are not immediately practical. Think of the times when you welcomed the sight of children playing in a playground without worrying about how to care for them. Think of moments when you beheld a waterfall without wondering about hydroelectric power. Or when you gazed into the eyes of a lover with no thought of

receiving anything for yourself. Or times in a church or forest when you experienced the loving presence of God without pondering consequences.

While we all have experienced this restful appreciation,
we often rush to practical applications and forget not only
that our children, waterfalls, and lovers are gifts from God
but that our love for them—this very experience of wordless
welcome—is a gift from God as well. It is the Spirit of God
active in us, rejoicing over the Word incarnate in history.
Recently I was listening to some particularly moving liturgical music in a church and wondered whether God was as
pleased as the congregation seemed to be. It struck me that
of course God is pleased; it is God's own pleasure that we
experience in our delight.[3]

Even when attending to the great threats to love, contemplation tends to rest rather than act immediately. There
are times when we rest in horror over violation of transcendent value. We stand aghast at human cruelty, without a
thought of doing anything. We feel our sense of transcendent
value tested to its limits when we witness death and suffering. We resonate with Jesus' question, "Father, why have
you forsaken me?"—particularly in the deadly silence that
follows. This too is contemplation. "We who possess the first-
fruits of the Spirit groan inwardly as we wait for our bodies
to be set free" (Rom 8:23).

In other words, there is a space in our consciousness
where we can rest in the truth. It is like breaking into a
clearing after thrashing through a forest. It is a time to stop
rather than plunge into the next thicket. Often this rest
brings with it a new orientation or a redirection of our efforts, and yet we are not stopping merely to plan. We can
stop sheerly to enjoy, to savor, to be grateful, or, on the
darker side, to be humbled by the reality of human weakness and to stand aghast at the depths of human malice.

5. Finally, the acts of realizing and appreciating are not
infallible. It is not always obvious that our delight or loath-

ing is from God, nor is it always the case. We are all egoists to some extent and like to think that our judgments are keen indicators of true value. For this reason we need the praxis of discerning the spirits. My conviction that the music I heard in church pleased God ought to be tempered by a readiness to discover mere sentimentality on my part. Or the horrors of someone's physical pain can often blind us to the worse horror of that person hating life, love, self, or God.

It is not only egoism that interferes with contemplative praxis. Our neuroses can create a straw self with artificial feelings and surrogate objects for those feelings. Our communities likewise tend to write the human drama for us, with its hidden taboos and idols that divert the eyes of our hearts. This is why we also need the praxis of discerning stories to uncover the biases that can infect contemplation.

The essence of contemplation, then, is not insight, not emotion, not imagination, not practical, and not infallible. It comprises rather the acts of realizing and appreciating. Although we all know what it means to dwell in loving appreciation of a flesh-and-blood friend, many find it difficult to stop like this when they are alone before the mystery of life and love. Many people who love God dearly do not always know how to be quiet and let their realizing and appreciating relish God and God's kind work. Perhaps it will help if we look more closely at what is involved in this realizing and appreciating. I am going to borrow the great expression of John Henry Newman—"a real assent"—to refer to the act of judgment that recognizes truth or value.[4]

## 3. REAL ASSENT

*I am the man who obscured your designs with my empty-headed words. I have been holding forth on matters I cannot understand, on marvels beyond me and my knowledge. I knew you then only by hearsay; but now, having seen you with my own eyes, I retract all I have said, and in dust and ashes I repent.*

Newman cites these words of Job (42:3–6) as an example of a real assent that ravaged acres of Job's mere notional assents. In notional assents we acknowledge the cogency, logic, and consistency of certain ideas or actions. Notional assents actually help our social gatherings gel because there is little at stake for us when we disagree on mere ideas. Schools, Newman says, tend to specialize in teaching mere notional assents, and homilies are often their showcases. Notional assents gather their materials not through personal experience but through hearsay, information, and belief.

Real assent, however, looks to *things,* not *notions.* "Till we have them, in spite of a full apprehension and assent in the field of notions, we have no intellectual moorings, and are at the mercy of impulses, fancies, and wandering lights, whether as regards personal conduct, social and political action, or religion."[5] In particular, for the truly spiritual person, "the Divine Word speaks of things, not merely of notions."

Often it takes some terribly rude treatment by life to shake a person out of an educated readiness for it all. "The mere popular preacher . . . the most awful truths are to him but sublime or beautiful conceptions. . . . But let his heart at length be ploughed by some keen grief or deep anxiety, and Scripture is a new book to him."

Here, at the heart of contemplation, we find the real goal of meditation. "The purpose, then, of meditation is to realize them; to make the facts which they relate stand out before our minds as objects, such as may be appropriated by a faith as living as the imagination which apprehends them." In other words, we meditate in order to get beyond the notions we need for meditation and to arrive at the reality of life, at things rather than ideas about things. This is why contemplation is considered a higher form of knowing than, indeed the perfection of, meditation alone.

There is an old saying that some writers and public speakers rely on: "Stick to the thing; the words will follow." In the effort to make a good case in public, there is no foolproof style of presentation or any list of convincing words or poignant metaphors to convey the truth effectively. Nor do lengthy analyses and clever deductions make much impression. Convincing talk springs rather from our personal realization about the reality in question. For the reality is always both the matter at hand and our own response to it as people ready to take a stand. Witness, not argument, makes for the most compelling speech.

Newman goes on to explain that while notional assents facilitate agreement between people, real assent often thwarts communication. This is because in a real assent the individual takes his or her own experience as a standard whose meaning, even when only partially understood, is significant for that individual in a way no other person can fully grasp. Indeed, the very essence of a real assent is a return to experience to validate a prospective judgment of fact or value, and no other person can do that for us.

But this does not mean that notional assents are basically political and real assents basically individualistic. Very much the contrary, real assents are the principle of political living because they have the power to persuade and inspire others far beyond the reasoning that appeals to consistency, coherence, or logic. Although notional assents may keep conversations pleasant, they do not affect people's conduct. Only people charged with the conviction born of experience carry the weight that directs minds and sways hearts.

These divisive and persuasive powers of real assent combined with the fact that only by real assent do we truly hear the gospel imply that the church must live in conflict. There are many kinds of conflict that damage the church, of course, but when the conflict regards the duty to explore the meaning of personal experience, we sin against the very spirit of truth that grasps the good news if we squelch this kind of dialog. Not that all real assents are valid. As I said, the realizations and evaluations proper to contemplation are not infallible. But they usually point to aspects of the mystery of life in this or that person's experience that ought to be respected in some fashion.

We can see how important it is, then, for retreat directors to know the difference between a real assent and a notional assent—and by "know" I do not mean "understand Newman's definition." Nor do I mean they should merely hold real assents in high esteem. I mean they should be able to recognize in themselves whether or not a real assent has occurred. They should explore what exactly happens when they realized some truth or appreciated some value. Without a personal grasp of the essence of a real assent, they will praise mere notions and by default protect the retreatant from a reality that, however harsh, always bears God's double Word to humanity.

The essence of a real assent is actually rather simple, so simple that many find it disturbing. *In a real assent, a person always returns to concrete data and finds them no longer perplexing but luminous.* What has occurred is that one's understanding of the data clarifies all the connections one has wondered about. The person's questions about the data at hand dry up, and the data then appear charged—or luminous—with the meaning and worth that she or he has realized.

For example, recall a time when you were humiliated in a way that you had to acknowledge was true—a time when somebody's remark put you in your place. The ego, cracking its whip over the intellect, opened up a number of alternative explanations to protect itself. But if none of the explanations fit the concrete experience, your questions dried up and, unless you are still bluffing yourself, you had to acknowledge the truth in a real assent. Then your memory of what you did or said becomes luminous with an honest shame. The data and their meaning appear as one.

True, some people stop wondering long before their questions are answered, and others keep wondering about details too insignificant in the total view of things. Real assents can come too early or too late. Likewise, we sometimes fear the power of raw data to push the truth in our face, or at other times we may have been so hypnotized by some former realization that we do not allow fresh data to revise our certitudes and convictions. It helps greatly, of course, to listen to the questions that other people raise and to hear them explain the grounds of their statements that X is true or Y is good. We can grow in the art of balanced judgment making.

This requirement that a real assent must return to the data explains why, in the *Spiritual Exercises* of Ignatius, the practice of using all five senses on a biblical scene was so highly regarded. It was not meant as an exercise in sentimentality, although no doubt that danger has always existed. Retreatants were expected first to recall the actual history of the event they were about to pray over. Then, only with the clear purpose of relishing the truth, of starting on the solid foundation of what actually happened,[6] they would give free rein to their imaginations in order to allow the concreteness of God's work in history to touch questions they could never articulate. And although most people today find it strange at first to enter into historical scenes through their imagination, the majority of those who try it find the practice surprisingly full of real assents.

The reduction of questions and the luminosity of the data are key features in how the first Christian disciples realized that Jesus was someone to be followed. Not that they had any abstract grasp of Christ's nature. But in their search for meaning in life and in their dissatisfaction with the legalisms of the religion of their day, they repeatedly discovered that the words and the person of Jesus laid their deepest questions to rest. "Blessed are you poor," Jesus said, and deep down most of them recognized how wholeheartedly they wanted this to be true. Peter put it all very succinctly when Jesus asked him if he was to go away: "Lord, to whom shall we go? You have the words of eternal life." Peter found in Jesus' words answers to questions about "eternal life" that he could hardly formulate, questions that nevertheless had badgered his religious consciousness for years.

Notice that we must talk about unformulatable questions that find answers. This is a very important phenomenon to notice about human wonder in general and about the spiritual life in particular. A text of Scripture will touch us; a kind word by a salesperson will edify us; a remark by some fictional character on TV will clarify something for us. In these kinds of experiences we rest with an answer to something we have wondered about but never explicitly. Our minds are actually full of questions, so full that we cannot begin to put them into words. (Will teachers ever learn to stop asking, "Are there any questions?" Far better to ask, "Now, what bothers you about what I've just said?" in order to surface some of the questions that students find difficult to formulate.) This is why it is crucially important for a retreat director to allow any and all kinds of observations to be spoken, provided they concern things or events and not just ideas. We simply must presume that the other person's spirit is in fact working wordlessly on profound issues.

A woman whom I was directing on a week's retreat came in to see me on the sixth day and announced, "It's all over." "You mean the retreat?" I said. "Not exactly," she said. "I just know now that God loves me." I asked her what happened, and she really couldn't say. Nor did she feel she had to do anything about it. All she knew was that she knew that God loves her. She told me she could end the retreat right there or go on for weeks; it didn't make any difference. It was a profoundly contemplative moment in which a jumble of unspoken questions about life found a single, simple answer in the realization that God actually loves her. It was a real assent, gathering many concrete experiences of worry, hope, illness, and love into an affirmation that dried up an enormous cluster of her questions—and many of her tears as well.

To speak practically, a helpful mentor will be aware that the retreatant has far more questions that can be expressed. It is these questions that form the main thread of a retreat, not some string of brilliant texts or beautiful metaphors. Many mentors have found that it makes little difference what text the retreatant uses for prayer; contemplation blossoms when retreatants discover a profoundly simple answer to a question they dared not speak. The criterion for choosing this or that text to pray over or when or where to pray is whatever is more conducive to tapping the lode of unexpressed questions about life and love within the person's heart. The mentor's task, therefore, includes listening for unexpressed questions and unresolved feelings in order to help the retreatant bring them into the light and decide whether they are worth pursuing. This requires some skill because it means turning an appreciative ear to what a retreatant is saying while turning a critical ear to what he or she cannot yet say.

In the next chapter on the praxis of deliberation we will return to this criterion for a real assent. A good decision, after all, stands or falls on the quality of the value judgment made by the person facing a choice. Therefore it will be crucial to notice the relevant questions—mostly unspoken—that a good choice lays to rest.

## 4. THE DYNAMICS OF REAL ASSENT

We have talked about the nature of a real assent—what exactly happens in us when we make one. But besides the nature of the act itself, there are conditions and implications that usually are present whenever we realize any truth or appreciate any value. Let us explore this dynamic by looking at a concrete example.

John is the chief executive of a large chain of grocery stores. He knows his business, and it thrives. However, he has been accused of hiring mostly part-time help, thus saving the company a great deal of money on the benefits that full-time employees would get. "But a lot of people need part-time jobs," he explains, "and we meet that need. Shall

I put a thousand part-time people out of work to employ three hundred full-time people?" A cogent argument: there really would be some injustice and insensitivity if he were to change his employment policy.

But then experience barges into his consciousness. His sister, now divorced and raising two children, has recently lost her job as a computer programmer and comes to him looking for work. He tells her that there are no full-time openings right now but that he can give her "several part-time" jobs. Furthermore, he says, he will find a way to give her the various health and retirement benefits she ordinarily would not get.

Slowly it dawns on him what he is doing. He is using his creativity to care for someone he loves. And he has been withholding that creativity from a thousand other men and women. Now he is bothered. Now he has questions about a fair hiring policy on the one hand and about his own creativity and love on the other. He can already feel the criticism of other grocery store owners who defend the no-part-time-benefits policy. He feels the managerial pull toward keeping things under control and yet, in the opposite direction, the gentler pull to take the risk of concrete love.

He has experienced a real assent to his sister's situation. His questions have dried up regarding his image of her needing work. For a while he was satisfied at having helped her out. Yet by realizing the value of job benefits for her in the concrete, new questions arose about his employees in general. He looks on these men and women in a very different light. The "data" of their working in check-out lines or the produce aisle impinge on his experience in a disturbing way.

Notice how a condition for a real assent is concrete love for someone or something. It was not until his sister felt the same financial insecurity that most of his employees feel that John could recognize the persons behind their question of benefits. But notice also that it is not merely concrete love for someone or something but the willingness to let that

love go beyond its familiar limits. John could have cared for
his sister's welfare in a loving way without giving a thought
to his employees. The normal condition for a real assent is
*concrete love for someone or something,* and the normal im-
plication of a real assent is *an expansion of the normal limits of our love.*

If we love the fullness of a person's or a community's
reality, if we love the fullness of God's reality, we are ready
for the entire truth. We are unafraid to pose the questions
that bother us. We do not build walls around our curiosity
when it envisions someone benefiting at our own cost. We
are not afraid of the long-range consequences of facing the
truth. We trust love. We are confident that our heart will
alert us to error and harm as they approach. And where we
fail, we trust the forgiving love in our community to make
up for our shortcomings.

When we allow love to move us, we do not necessarily
give more of ourselves to others. Paradoxically, we first receive something from them, no matter how poverty-stricken
they may be. When we open our hearts to love, we allow a
flood of questions in, their questions, questions we do not
readily welcome, questions that were not ours but become
ours as we expand our concerns to include the concerns of
others. It is these new questions that bring us to the brink
of realization and appreciation. It is in identifying with specific people—from infants to the elderly, from the unborn to
the dead and forgotten—that we inherit the wealth of God's
Kingdom. It is a treasure house brimming with the questions, concerns, hopes, anxieties, delights, and griefs of our
neighbor.

John's heart now moves back and forth between the contemplation that realizes the concrete meaning of his love to
the meditation that seeks to understand all the ramifications involved. Yet if he follows his best instincts, he will
more frequently rest in the contemplative moment where he
simply realizes, "Yes, I do love these people; it is true; I
cannot deny it." It is likely that he will then realize, "Yes, I

know I am going to extend some sort of benefits to them—
what, I do not know yet—but it will happen."

On the one hand, contemplation has a destructive power
regarding ideas that do not make sense of concrete experience. The fact that real assents tend to demolish the fences
of our love probably accounts for why we so cling to mere
notional assents. A good mentor will be careful to avoid the
seemingly harmless chitchat about good ideas. And where
a retreatant frequently returns to mere speculation or information, she provides a major clue that she is afraid to
look at some specific personal experience. Pride, or vulner-
ability, knows how merciless the truth can be.

On the other hand, contemplation has a conservative
effect regarding the ideas that have made sense of concrete
experience. A wise pastor puts more stock in contemplation
than in insight, preferring reality to mere bright ideas.
That is, he or she habitually takes the time to realize the
exact nature of a situation, particularly all the battles that
lay behind present achievements, all the wounds left over
from the past, and all the hopes for the future that lay hidden in the hearts of a congregation. Better an inefficient
church council comprising people who know their past than
an efficient council with no memory. Better a messy liturgy
enacted by men and women who accept each other's limita-
tions than a textbook liturgy performed by actors.

But beyond its destructive and conservative powers,
contemplation is ultimately a creative force. To see this, we
must consider the purpose of contemplation in the context
of a retreat.

## 5. THE PURPOSE OF CONTEMPLATION

What has contemplation to do with "withdrawing
from immediate concerns to assess and integrate our
relationships"?

Generally speaking, the answer is obvious. Contemplation clinches the truth. And good choices should be based on

the truth, as far as possible. But recall how meditation came both before and after a choice. Before a choice meditation aims at understanding how love and its failures brought about the concrete situation one finds oneself in. After a choice meditation aims at understanding how that love-inspired choice may make a real difference to one's situation. Before the choice the task is to *assess* one's relationships. After the choice, the task is to *integrate* the relationships affected by the choice.

Contemplation plays a similar double role, sandwiched between these two phases of meditation. In an ascensional mode we move from noticing to meditation to contemplation of how things actually stand in our world. At the apex, where we rest in a loving vision of the needs and potentialities around us, we make our choice. Then in a returning mode we contemplate (that is, we realize and appreciate) the meaning of our choice, we meditate on its concrete ramifications, and then notice what adaptations are needed in specific times and places.

So in a retreat we contemplate not only the sins and graces in a situation, we contemplate the move we have chosen to respond to that situation. Choices, if they are of any significance, affect the entire pattern of our relationships to friends, work, self, environment, and God. Before rushing to put our choice into effect, then, there is a need to contemplate the integration tasks of a retreat. Concretely this means realizing and appreciating how God's inner Word and God's outer Word act with us in our decision. It means recognizing and appreciating the likely effects of our choice on all the levels of our life. It is not yet planning—that is the task of meditation. Rather, it is welcoming and relishing the truth that we incarnate Christ and are quickened by the Spirit in our return to action.

In the old terminology of the spiritual life, we have reached the unitive way, not as a permanent rank of holiness but simply as an experience regarding the decision we have made. We have not made the decision alone, and we will not carry it out alone. In *Spiritual Exercises for Today* we contemplate in this way during the Third and Fourth Weeks. In the Third Week we join Christ in his passion for the salvation of Jerusalem; we share his agony and his compassion for others as we envision the relationships we have altered through the choice we made. We also share, in the Fourth Week, the joy of Jesus that the Reign of God is indeed arriving at a specific time and place, both among his disciples and, we hope, among the people to whom we are returning.[7]

It is this second phase—the return phase—of a retreat that makes the *Spiritual Exercises* of Ignatius radically different from the many "spiritual exercises" before him. From Plotinus to Ignatius, Christian spirituality was dominated by the ideal of ascending to God through contemplation. From Ignatius on, that ideal was complemented by our loving descent with God back to earth to bring the good news of Salvation to our neighbors. The Christian does not rest at the apex of contemplation. Rather, Ignatius expected that a concrete choice be made—a choice that, in union with God's inner and outer Words, would mark the breaking in of the Kingdom upon the world.

Contemplation, therefore, has a double purpose. It lifts us up to see what is true and good, as well as what is false and evil. Then it turns our appreciative eye to where God looks, to look with God, to be the mouth and hands of God who desires to be incarnate in history's every moment.

This is why it is very important not to end a retreat with the decision. As far as possible, move toward the decision in the middle of the retreat, so that the heart may take the time to savor the ramifications of the decision with the taste buds of God, as it were.

## 6. THE PINNACLE OF CONTEMPLATION

It would be unwise to end this discussion of contemplation by speaking of the purpose of contemplation. That would leave the impression that contemplation is sheerly a means to an end—in our case, some ultimately practical purpose. But, despite Thomas Aquinas's dictum that "every agent acts for an end," there is some question whether Aristotle, on whom he depends, thought that all such ends lie beyond the acts of the agent. Aristotle distinguished between the productive arts, in which the means / end distinction clearly applies, and the performing arts, in which it does not. A flute maker's work is a means to an end beyond itself, but the flute player's playing is the playing.[8] Here we return to the more classical insights of Plato, Aristotle, and Plotinus, for whom the mind was naturally made to find rest in contemplation of what is beautiful, real, and valuable.

The pinnacle of contemplation is, as one ought to expect by now, the realization and appreciation of the concrete meaning of love for whatever is absolute—the one we call God. It is true that our minds and hearts naturally seek the truth and value what is absolute, but as long as we belong to history, we cannot grasp, let alone rest in for long, that absolute. We can only intimate its presence beyond the partial truths and values we do grasp, and intimate its power in our very nature to seek it. So it is that we find ourselves loving what we experience very concretely yet do not grasp. We do take great spiritual pleasure in simply realizing this truth of our souls and in appreciating the One who is source and object of our love precisely while we experience that love springing from unknown depths within us and carrying us beyond all known objects.

To the question *Who are you?* we rest content with what we have realized about the concrete meaning of our love. We delight in the truth that the source of our love is a Someone with kind purposes. We also take great spiritual pleasure in realizing and appreciating the unfathomable worth of another person or a full community of persons. While we do not attribute to others, not even to ourselves, our very capacity for love (as we do to God), we do acknowledge that the same bottomless capacity exists in them. So we realize and appreciate in persons an absolute, something that at least in principle is without limits. And if this datum of experience were not enough, Jesus lifted an obscure commandment from Leviticus (17:3) on loving one's neighbor to a rank alongside the greatest commandment to love God with all one's heart and soul. Even though this complicates the metaphysics of means and ends, the Christian doctrine of love generally refuses to make love of neighbor a mere means to some end that excludes the neighbor.

Augustine called love the "gravity of my soul." Just as physical objects will fall until they land and rest, so the soul, by its love, will continue to move until it rests in its beloved. There is a happy coincidence in the fact that modern physics has relativized the metaphor of gravity just as modern Scripture studies have relativized the ideal of an earthly love that does not move. Bodies in motion will stay in motion, as long as no outside force intervenes. The earth is constantly falling toward but missing the sun, sailing in a felicitous equilibrium of gravity and centrifugal force. Those who love God are directed not only to return that love but also to love the neighbor with that love in a moving equilibrium of the two great commandments.

The pinnacle of contemplation, therefore, is a loving gaze upon God, with the ready expectation to discover God giving that love with which we love, both in our hearts and in our history. It is indeed a high point, but while God continues to walk in history and to inspire human hearts, the pinnacle is not the trail's end. The very God we cherish is on the move and draws us with gentle cords to join in that intimate outpouring of love. To discover the path along which God draws us, we do not rest forever at the peak. Inspired by God's Spirit, and emulating God's Word, we soon turn our attention to the deliberation necessary to make a good choice.

# CHAPTER EIGHT

# The Praxis of Deliberation

The malls, schools, ads, and catalogs of a developed country present its citizens with so many insignificant decisions that the very nature of making a truly significant decision is obliterated. What we usually focus on is how our decisions change our surroundings. But in making or buying products, giving or receiving services, even in speaking and hearing words, human decisions not only rearrange an environment, they gradually and imperceptibly remake each person making the decision.

The situation is not essentially different among those in dire want. When a community spends its creative energies chiefly on finding food and shelter, the minds of its people are prey to the illusion that products are all that count in life. We have all seen how greed is no stranger to the formerly poor. It was to the crowds who had already eaten their fill of bread that Jesus warned, "Do not work for food that cannot last."

We can be so hypnotized by our power over nature and over other people—benign power as well as its opposite—that we spend a lifetime trying to make our mark on the memories of others without any thought of the marks we are making on ourselves. History can become reduced in our minds to a succession of spectacles to be celebrated or condemned by others similarly tempted to make achievement and production the sole measures of life. Even people of high moral standards are often so entranced by the permanent possibility of producing a better social order that they fail to savor the taste of the lives they actually live.

## 1. DECISION: THE LINK BETWEEN SPIRIT AND HISTORY

To grasp the nature of human decisions in a way that envisions their effect on ourselves as well as on our environs, we can think of decision as *the link between spirit and history*. I mean spirit and history in their very concrete senses. Meaningful history is not a measured chronology. It is not even the account of a people written by the historian. The historian's book merely points toward the actual events that constitute history. That actual history is an interconnected flow of specifically human events—the surprising initiatives, the responses to unforeseen problems, and all the failures in initiative and response stemming from weakness or malice. This is the history that historians investigate and, to a modest extent, elucidate.

On the side of spirit, the events of human consciousness are not mere subjective experiences. Nor are psychologists, counselors, and spiritual mentors interested merely in understanding how the events of consciousness relate to one another. Through human decision, including the failure of decision, subjective meanings become common meanings that condition the lives of others and impart a thrust to the trajectory of history.

Decision, spirit, and history, consequently, are mutually defining. Those who regard history without its roots in spirit end up absolving everyone of the horrors of war, mass starvation, decayed cities, and the like. History seems to run on a Hegelian "cunning of Reason," which manipulates our wits for purposes beyond our ken.[1] By contrast, those who regard spirit without its ramifications in history run the Augustinian danger of stripping human decision of any intelligible effect on our common life. Then the quality of a decision seems to depend merely on personal virtue, consistency, or sheer daring rather than on responsible stewardship for the earth God loves.

Concretely this means that our decisions are always about *authority*. When we deliberate over options, we are deliberating over our own authorship, on our public responsibility for the world at hand. For many it means courageously taking on authority for a situation that begs attention. For others it means the more humbling decision to yield authority to another when it becomes obvious that one's effectiveness has run its course. For still others the decision may hinge on finding a new way to share authority with spouse, children, employees, or employers. More than ever before in history, retreatants in today's democratic societies are confronted by decisions either to wield or relinquish authority.

You will remember our definition of a retreat: a withdrawal from immediate concerns to assess and integrate our relationships. We should not focus strictly on ourselves alone nor strictly on some project we might undertake or friend to care for. It is the living relationship between ourselves and a career or a friend or a community that we change in every decision we make. By addressing the issue of our authority, we avoid separating the "objective" and "subjective" effects of any decision. The change in the one who makes the decision is just as "objective," in the sense of being actual or true, as the changes in his or her surroundings. Even when circumstances prevent us from carrying out some decision, we have already created something new, something "objective" insofar as we changed our own hearts by a commitment, making us different persons than we were before.

By keeping our focus on the authoritative relationships we bear rather than the effects or products we bring about, we escape the fiction of an isolated self looking over options as if they were ducks in a shooting gallery. We entertain the permanent possibility that the shooter may be mad. The praxis of deliberation, therefore, will be much more objective, much less distorted by bias, if we think of the decision we intend to make as simultaneously altering both our own spirit and the history we are a part of.

Every decision is like this whether or not anyone adverts to it. Philosophically every decision is a decision to re-create a person-in-community-in-history. Theologically every decision is a decision for or against the City of God, of which we are each citizens.

In previous chapters we looked at various dimensions of the praxis that leads up to effective commitment in the Reign of God—imagining, noticing, meditating, and contemplating. Now, as we arrive at the final issue of deliberating, we face a number of questions. What role do feelings play? Common wisdom advises that we trust our feelings, yet common experience tells us that not all feelings are trustworthy. Also, one's wherewithal to make a good decision depends to a great extent on one's moral development. Yet how can a person develop morally except by making good decisions? And, finally, how free are we to make a decision when we also believe that God has divine purposes for us?

These questions are felt keenly by people facing a commitment, although not necessarily in these somewhat philosophical terms. It is important to realize that we are not trying to create a theory of decision that purports to describe how every person makes a decision. Rather, we are pointing to some of the possible dynamics that may be at work in decision making and posing questions that may be helpful to keep in mind; that is, we are enriching our praxis of deliberation by understanding the kinds of questions that decision making usually raises.

## 2. FEELINGS: PRELUDE TO A CHOICE

It is difficult to imagine ourselves making a decision we have no feelings about. Feelings are our early indicators of value. Love and hate, desire and aversion, joy and sadness[2] arise in us spontaneously, alerting us to the worth of persons, projects, art, music, cities, and anything else on which we pass judgment. Yet feelings are not to be equated with value judgments. Just as insights indicate intelligibility but only judgment affirms that intelligibility, so feelings indicate value but only a judgment affirms the value in question. Considered in their cognitive function, feelings are questions regarding value.

It is very important, therefore, that we be in touch with our feelings, since they alert us to issues that need evaluation. But contrary to common belief, to "be in touch" with our feelings does not require that our affectivity be particularly strong or demonstrative. "Being in touch" requires not affective but cognitive work. It means being perceptive about inner experience, raising questions about the feelings we notice, and verifying what we think is going on in us. In my experience, "feeling" types of people are no more in touch with their feelings in this sense than "thinking" types.

The reason this intellectual work on our feelings is so important is that both our feelings and their objects can be unknown. For example, have you ever discovered that you were jealous? Normally jealousy festers in us long before we realize it. We look askance at somebody intruding upon a friend of ours. We honestly believe that the intruder is rude or unfair or unsuited to our friend's high standards (by which we are deemed eminently suitable). Then the truth dawns. It is not fear for our friend we are feeling; it is anger at the intruder. The feeling of jealousy has influenced our behavior, and we failed to notice it. These kinds of revelations about our own affectivity go on all the time. People who are "in touch" with their feelings tend to know what they are feeling because they first tend to *wonder* about them. At any given time they are quite aware that there are areas where they do not know what they feel, but they keep the question alive.

Furthermore, being in touch with one's feelings means not only wondering about which feeling one experiences but what the object of that feeling really is. In our example, we mistook both the feeling and its true object: we were feeling anger (not fear), and our feelings were directed toward the interloper (not our friend).

Finally, even after we make a significant decision, there remains the task of adapting our feelings to the new direction the decision sets. The praxis of deliberation should also take into account the effects of a possible decision on one's feelings for the future.

Here then are three valuable questions a mentor in a retreat can raise: (1) Is X really the feeling you are experiencing? (2) Is Y really what X is directed toward? and (3) How would you feel after choosing option Z?

These clarifications are preliminary to making a decision, of course, and they are essential. Feelings have great power to channel our notice either toward or away from an object even when we are unaware of them. Because of this the mentor may wear the hat of a psychological analyst for a time.

## 3. THE AMBIGUITY OF FEELINGS

When the feelings are clarified, the cognitive work of understanding ends. Yet there is a further important question that normally follows: Shall I trust this feeling? Here we move from our cognitive need to know our feelings to the moral need to trust them. We move from what to should. We move from analysis to seeking counsel.

Suddenly we find ourselves in a kind of vicious circle. We may feel drawn to participate, say, in an anti-abortion demonstration. Yet we also feel afraid of this attraction. In other words, we have a feeling about a feeling, with no access in feelings themselves to a higher court of appeal to determine which feeling is more trustworthy. In practice we usually seek advice from people whose integrity we trust—

yet even here our very trust in others has deep roots in our ambivalent feelings about them.

My point here is that feelings alone are unreliable guides to what is objectively good. Just because I desire a comfortable life does not mean it is worth desiring. And just because I am sad about losing my reputation does not mean the loss is necessarily bad for me. As we have already seen in our discussion of praxis and noticing, there are pulls and counterpulls in us that demand vigilance and discernment. But the very readiness for discernment requires a prior realization that the objectively good is not necessarily what feels good.

The realization that there is a difference between objective worth and mere attraction—indeed, that there is even such a thing as objective worth that lies beyond subjective attitudes—is a major and fundamental realization, of course. It is not a judgment on any particular person or project; rather, it is a change in the very criterion by which we make all our value judgments. We make the personal discovery that the standard by which we evaluate anything is something beyond mere like and dislike, desire and aversion, joy and sadness. It is a conversion of our moral praxis. It calls for a new asceticism rooted in our personal commitment to the good rather than mere obedience to laws, to the expectations of others, or to the anarchical principle "If it feels good, do it."

## 4. CONSCIENCE: ARBITER OF VALUES

If feelings only raise the question of value without providing an answer, by what criteria do we decide to take one path and not another?

There are a number of different considerations that we actually make. For example, we weigh the pros and cons, assessing as best we can which option makes the most sense for the most people. Often this seems enough to determine the best path; one option simply makes more sense than all other known options. But more often than not the various paths have mixtures of merits and shortcomings that we cannot easily compare.

To explore each path in depth it is not enough to assess the outcomes of our decisions or the projected goals we had in mind. We should also scrutinize whether or not we are borrowing value judgments rather than taking the authority to make our own. Youngsters, of course, borrow almost all their value judgments from others, until the day comes when they begin to test inherited mores and taboos for validity. Adults, on the other hand, usually embrace some tradition, but it is difficult to tell whether that embrace is the result of taking personal authority for continuing what is best in a tradition or is just the result of fearing to question one's tradition.

To sort out values that may be borrowed out of fear or a need to belong, it helps to distinguish three "voices" that we normally hear when we face a decision: (1) the apparent needs of a specific situation; (2) the expectations of one's culture, family, and friends; (3) the standards of one's tradition, belief system, and principles. These voices often disagree with each other. Imagine an elderly man with cancer who must decide about chemotherapy. (1) The technology of chemotherapy is at hand in the local hospital. (2) His family feels strongly invested in prolonging his life, so the need for chemotherapy seems obvious. (3) Still, he may hear a weak voice from some tradition about "no extraordinary means" and find that it touches something he wants to explore.

Sometimes it may seem as though one of these "voices" is completely silent, but we should not be fooled. Most of our moral stands are inherited, and many of them have never been tested in the concrete. We need both to hear the various voices explicitly and to test them for validity. This is why it helps to talk about them aloud to another person: we only really hear the "voice" when we actually voice what we hear.

These various techniques for clarifying all the values involved in a decision are only an early step in the praxis of deliberation. A retreatant receives a valuable service when the mentor explores these competing values explicitly. Unfortunately, many people, particularly "moral" educators, so dote on "values clarification" that they give the impression that good decisions pop out of the process like a cake from an oven. They completely ignore the complex task of prioritizing the clarified values. In fact, it is far easier to clarify one's values than to commit oneself to one and not another. This is the task of conscience.

Here we should note the difference between conscience and feelings, since they are made partly of the same stuff but perform different functions. Feelings are relatively spontaneous and specific responses to what seems good or bad. Conscience is the experience of the entire drift of a large body of both thoughts and feelings. It is an awareness of one's own self as being pulled or stayed by both thoughts and feelings.

The criterion of conscience, therefore, is a felt harmony among our feelings, thoughts, and self-image. And by "felt harmony" I mean not exactly the presence of some peaceful aura but, more precisely, *the absence of the disturbing questions and feelings that other options tend to unleash.* The "peaceful aura" is, in its essence, simply the absence of relevant questions, including the "questions" represented by disturbing feelings. We might imagine Saint Matthew leaving his tax collector's desk without a look back because in Jesus his deepest desires were met and his deepest fears were healed.

Conscience today suffers a bad reputation, particularly when seen with its cousin, guilt feelings. It is often not easy to tell whether disturbing questions and feelings are remnants of a childhood superego or really represent an adult intuition that something is wrong. In "Conscience and Superego"[3]—one of those articles one returns to often—John Glaser draws fine phenomenological descriptions of a mature conscience and of its atavistic imitator, the superego. The superego, he says, works on the principle that one must make oneself lovable. We can see how the superego is formed if we look at how children relate to adults. Children so desperately fear the withdrawal of love that they devise surprisingly clever schemes, ranging from rigid obedience to rampant disobedience, to ensure that parental figures will not abandon them. The value of anything is centrally linked to maintaining a relationship to authorities, even if it means accepting punishment, which is a form of payment for belonging.

As children grow up their genuine conscience begins to be formed when they fall in love and discover a world where the value of things is linked also to the welfare of others. Ideally, their need to belong is usurped by their desire to care for others. But the superego never fully dies, and so its voice continues to echo far into adult years.

There are several clues that indicate mere superego and not genuine conscience. One is that we atomize units of activity instead of seeing them as part of a larger process. The "shoulds" we feel seem to derive from some list of forbidden deeds rather than from a responsible assessment of the many factors involved in a concrete situation. When we experience guilt feelings about certain deeds without seeing what bearing they have on people we care for—including ourselves considered in the full context of our lives—we can suspect our need to feel acceptable is giving the orders.

Another telltale sign of the superego is the absence of any creativity in doing good. Our consciousness is centered on maintaining some "good" in the exact form in which we have envisioned it rather than exploring adaptations of old principles or wholly new avenues for bringing life to others. This does not feel so much like "guilt feelings" as "moral maintenance," yet it likely stems from the same source: our need to be considered worthy to belong. With a robust conscience, by contrast, our consciousness is centered on creating something "good" that is appropriate to a concrete situation, and it gathers the resources of our imagination and insight instead of ignoring them.

## 5. THE LIMITS OF CONSCIENCE

Conscience, therefore, is a higher moral principle than feelings, values clarification, or the voice of the superego. Yet conscience itself has its own limits. Not only is "doing good" insufficient as a life goal for most people, it is also quite difficult to accomplish by goodwill alone. I would like to discuss the limits of conscience in three areas: moral relativism, moral impotence, and moral fear.

*Moral Relativism.* If you recall from chapter 5, both a good conscience and a bad conscience follow the same rule: Affectivity and imagination tend to maintain a moral horizon while thoughts and reflection tend to question it. In people going from good to better, their heart takes the lead, while any fears or hesitations they experience usually stem from too much analysis, or from seemingly good ideas that appeal merely to their sense of order. In people going from bad to worse, their heart also takes the lead as their misguided love of power or pleasure drives them on, while their conscience stings them with considerations of fairness, reason, and long-range consequences.[4]

In other words, a lax conscience can feel as much subjective harmony as a sensitive one. We can imagine Judas, before the crucifixion, as "peaceful" with his calculations. Just because a person is unbothered by questions does not mean there are not serious questions that could be raised.

Even for sensitive consciences there will be different interpretations of "what makes sense," on account of the ambiguities deriving from their imaginal theology of history. As we saw in chapter 4, "what makes sense" depends heavily on how a person envisions history. In the preservative vision the best option will be whatever maximizes maintaining the values of the past. In the interruptive, it will be whatever maximizes trust in God or in fate. In the progressive, whatever improves things. And in the dialectical, whatever seems to represent the honest struggle for life—an image vulnerable to the most destructive interpretations itself.

*Moral Impotence.* Not only can conscience alone not evaluate its own horizon, it cannot always carry out the good it recognizes. A common mythical expectation about retreats suggests that we should explore several paths to determine which is most for the glory of God and the good of the neighbor, on the presumption that once this path is revealed, we will take it. While sometimes there is indeed a task of discovering that path, the more serious problem is that we do not take it once we see it.

Saint Paul wrote the classic Christian statement on our radical frigidity. "I cannot understand my own behavior. I fail to carry out the things I want to do, and I find myself doing the very things I hate" (Rom 7:15). Saint Augustine contemplated his finger, how it moved whenever he willed, but how his will to be celibate would not move when he willed.[5] Very often this impotence shows in our inability *not* to retaliate for some wrong done to us. The essential problem is not that we cannot see what is best; it is that we are unable to do it. We need an energy that we cannot muster on our own to do good and avoid evil.

The mind will hardly stand for this radical embarrassment. So it often happens that we suppress what we know is the best decision and undertake a prolonged search for some alternative. But every alternative leaves conscience more or less uneasy, and so we break camp and continue the search again. Gradually we come to believe that God does not care or that God has died, leaving us to wander aimlessly without the directions home. And the more we search, the weaker our memories of our moral impotence become; we forget the time when we saw the good path and could not bring ourselves to take it.

In most cases the right path is not difficult to perceive. Granted, it may not appear immediately, and perhaps we cannot see where the path will lead. But we should not let this perceptual fog blind us to the motivational problem that we cannot get our legs to walk without God's help.

Often the most contrite people—people with a keen sense of their failures and with firm purposes of amendment—never face their moral powerlessness. They count on guilt to cover their moral poverty. They act as though taking the blame for something they didn't do were preferable to humbly admitting they never had the power to do it. Usually it is only as they approach a major decision or a deeper commitment that they discover to their shock that they cannot really make the best move simply by wanting to.

It is the healthiest shock in the spiritual life, and it normally has to jolt us over and over again. Of all the "real assents" necessary to living in love with God, the realization that I commonly fail to carry out what I choose, and that I do the things I hate, has the greatest power to turn us to God. Alcoholics Anonymous keeps this principle at the core of its teaching—that we must admit our own powerlessness and surrender to a "higher power."

This is why the central attitude of a person making a fundamental change in life ought to be a combination of *begging* and *gratitude*. We can easily find analogies in the New Testament of men and women begging Jesus to heal their blindness and to free them to walk. But we need to remain in the tension of simultaneously receiving the power to walk the path we have chosen and begging to receive the power to continue walking.

The mentor ought to be alert to any dodging of this impotence. If the typical ploy is to rush into a phony kind of discernment, one that pretends ignorance about what is best, then before entering into a deliberation process, it is crucial to determine whether any deliberation is really necessary. What may be necessary is merely the humility to admit that something in us holds us back from giving God our all and that we are passionless by ourselves to do anything about it. No doubt we must take a retreatant's self-revelations seriously. But we should also take seriously the question whether the person is deeply trapped in the illusion that "I intend to do the right thing; I just I don't know what it is!"

*Moral Fear.* Finally, besides moral relativism and moral impotence, conscience suffers from moral fear. We are afraid because despite our best deliberations, we can never be sure we are doing what is best. We fear, on the one hand, to let go of our securities and our grievances and to fall into the hands of the living God. On the other, we fear our own self-centeredness and its devious ways of infecting the good we do. Jesus was patently afraid as he faced the cross, surely not only because of death but more deeply because he feared he may have overlooked some alternative way to precipitate the Reign of God, "praying that, if it were possible, this hour might pass him by" (Mk 14:35).

Women and men of mature conscience experience moral fear every day. They know well their own selfishness, and so they fear that what others may praise about them is just disguised egotism. They fear that their love for others falls far too short of their heart's desire. They fear for their families, for their countries, for the globe, knowing that politicians and their advisers are attracted by the desire for power and fame at least as much as by care for the common good. They fear because no one knows how good any given age in history really is and so people must hope without apparent grounds. Most of all, they quake before God in a way that blends profound reverence with existential terror.

It is not unhealthy for a retreat mentor to recognize this fear and not cover it over too quickly with pious reassurances. Particularly in the teeth of a major decision, a retreatant can be gripped by the fear that this is all a big mistake, that there is no way to be sure this is the right step, and so on. Like admitting our moral immobility, it leaves us begging God for . . . for what? Not certitude; the experienced conscience knows better than to expect to know for certain what God desires. Not even conviction; as if firm resolve were naturally available in our fragile hearts. But *assurance:* that even an uncertain, weak-hearted, mustard-seed-sized decision has the power to bring about God's Reign. Particularly in a retreat situation, it is important that a mentor not give much verbal assurances. A mentor is not a parent but a guide bringing a retreatant before the living God. And when the retreatant receives the grace of *assurance* directly from God, no words from a mentor could ever have the power of the divine hope that God personally bequeaths.

Since there clearly are people with well-formed consciences, there must be some higher criterion that forms conscience itself, that thaws its frigidity, and assures it that God's hand is not stayed by human uncertainty. Moral relativism, moral impotence, and moral fear cannot be the end of the story. That higher criterion is, of course, being in love.

## 6. BEING IN LOVE

Throughout this entire discussion of the many facets of spiritual praxis, we have been building a spiritual anthropology—a model of person-in-community-in-history. It is not a set of ideals to achieve or recipes for becoming a spiritual person. Rather, it is a sketch of the dynamics that go on in all of us whether or not we notice it. Granted, by understanding the many spiritual events we experience, certain norms come to light, but readers should regard the norms not as my directives for their behavior but as personal discoveries they might make—discoveries that form the ground on which to stand with authority.

My point here is that as we now turn our attention to the workings of love in human consciousness, we are not *prescribing* a remedy for the ills of conscience. No, we are investigating the remedy that is already there. In fact, part of the difficulty of recognizing that conscience depends on love is the very presence of love in people who have, by and large, been liberated to follow their heart.

In other words, despite all the difficulties in noticing, envisioning, meditating, contemplating, and deliberating, we must acknowledge that these operations take place in a person more or less in love. Our being in love makes a world of difference in how our spiritual praxis actually occurs.

To some degree we praise the healing power of human love. A child from a happy family is functionally more intelligent and realistic than an equally capable child from an unhappy family. An adult in love is enabled to find the delicate balance of conflicting responsibilities more easily than an adult gripped by fear or hatred. Human love can, to a great extent, lift us beyond our moral horizons. It can energize us to show in our deeds what is shining in our minds. It strips our fears of their menacing power.

Perhaps to a lesser degree we praise the power of our love for God. Recall what was said in chapter 1 about where we derive meaning for the term *God*. We hear what our parents and teachers say about God, and it stirs something in our hearts. The universe becomes a different, more welcoming place. At the same time, within our hearts we experience a love that consistently goes beyond all the things, people, and communities that we love. It is common experience that when we turn to God (or at least to a "higher power") as a "you" and lay before God our moral insufficiency, we usually see the good that needs doing, feel the courage to do it, and lose our fear of what is to come.

Still, not everyone trusts their experiences of loving God. Just as a moral conversion is necessary to go beyond mere feelings to conscience, so an affective, or religious, conversion is necessary to go beyond mere conscience to effective reliance on one's love for the transcendent to provide the wisdom, power, and courage with which to meet life. That conversion will contrast strongly with any romantic, nationalistic, or self-centered versions of "true-love" that we may have been living with. It puts our life on a new and, at first, strange footing. What usually happens when we yield to this divine pull on our hearts?

Saint Paul noted that when we are in love with God we experience three gifts of faith, charity, and hope. While there has been little disagreement that these three form a basic triad in the spiritual life, only recently have we asked how they function psychologically in the individual and how this individual functioning brings about the Reign of God in history.

*Faith is the eye of the heart.* When our consciousness is fundamentally oriented toward the love of God, of God's Reign, and of the people God has surrounded us with (including ourselves), we much more quickly see what is worthwhile in any given situation. We more easily stand outside our own egoisms and discover an objectivity that regards the largest possible good. Faith, then, is first of all about concrete value judgments. It was faith that prompted the first Christian disciples to recognize something of absolute value in Jesus. It was faith that enabled them to recognize the pearl of great price in the good news. It was faith that held them near Jesus even as their fears and confusion mounted. Ultimately it was faith that empowered them to see the value of Jesus' death and to recognize the reality and meaning of his Resurrection.

From the judgments of value held by a people in love with God come judgments of fact about reality. It is part of our natural bent to make our worldview consistent with what we think is most precious about life. The essential truths we hold, therefore, are indicated by such propositions as "The Reign of God is at hand!" "I am with you all days, unto the end of time," "You have one in you who is greater than anyone in the world." Having realized these truths, early Christians raised the obvious question, Who is this that the wind and sea obey him? But, although the question of Jesus' status vis-à-vis God certainly occurred during New Testament times, it was centuries before Christians could adequately formulate the propositions about his divinity and present them in creeds that we hold "in faith," not as a blind test of orthodoxy but primarily as much-needed anchors for a consistent worldview that values love above all.

Indeed, when we no longer *feel* strongly about the values to which our faith assents—for example, to return good for evil—it helps immensely to cling to the truth that "the Lord is very near—there is no need to worry" (Phil 4:5). We saw above that feelings are ambiguous indicators of value. By recognizing in ourselves the phenomenon that our love reveals values that feelings do not, we discover the great emotional educator in our hearts; that is, we find that errant feelings can be taught to recognize what is worthwhile under the tutelage of love. It is a school that does not spare the rod, however, as anyone can attest who has suffered the dark nights of the soul when feelings have either revolted against their teacher or skipped school altogether.

Fortunately, it is surprisingly easy to tell whether a person is acting in love or not, provided that the mentor knows the experience personally, of course. Indeed, there seems to be a "grace of office" that goes with spiritual mentoring. When a retreatant enters the room for a conference, the mentor very often experiences a love for God that floods his or her heart with wisdom. The mentor easily notices whether the retreatant acts like a "we" with God looking at the concrete situation or like an "I" trying somewhat fearfully to please God by moral behavior. The mentor can almost smell whether the concerns that arise are chiefly the individual's or truly part of God's concern, particularly as manifested in the church at large.

Of course, a "grace of office" typically stays in the office. The minute the mentor or retreatant leaves the office, the mentor is left with a more raw faith on which to live her or his own life. But that very faith is enough to recognize that the absence of spiritual consolation is no less a share in the life of Jesus and the Spirit bringing about the Reign of God in one's own time and place.

*Charity is effective love.* Charity is not an automatic payoff of faith. Saint Paul recognized that even the faith that moves mountains is nothing without charity. In other words, Christians may experience the wisdom of faith without the power of charity. If we are to acknowledge that charity is itself a gift of God and not merely a natural outcome of faith, it seems appropriate to associate it with the empowerment we receive to overcome our moral frigidity. When we beg for the grace to do what we know is right—or not do what we know is wrong—we are asking for the power of love to prompt us or stay us.

If faith is the eye of love, then charity is the guts to love. Both are gifts, each to be sought as we feel their lack. According to Saint Paul, the object of our charity is the neighbor, not God. We love the neighbor with God's own gift and power of love. But while the gestures of charity praised in the Bible are largely toward individuals, we should not overlook the great love Jesus had toward Jerusalem as representing God's entire chosen people. In other words, we need the power to act lovingly for the common good as much as toward any individual.

Furthermore, in this age where we recognize the enormity of abuse in families and how it brings individuals to hate their own selves, it seems timely to include a healthy self-love within charity's ambit. Indeed, we can find the most patent examples of our inability to love effectively in how we treat ourselves. Many otherwise religious men and women detest their own bodies or spirits, either on account of psychological trauma or because of demeaning social judgments. For the wounded in our society a retreat can be a privileged time to beg the grace of charity toward oneself. By this I mean asking for the courage to take genuine care of oneself.

*Hope is confident desire.* Just as we can experience the gift of faith without charity, so we can experience both of them without the gift of hope. This happens when we are gripped by a fear of outcomes. There are two chief reasons why we might fear outcomes. One, of course, is the intractable prevalence of evil in our world. For all the good people actually accomplish, evil seems to match and often surpass it. So even where we know the good to do (faith) and go ahead and do it (charity), we can remain skeptical that the world will ever progress historically toward a better approximation to the Reign of God.

We do not have to be taught to fear the power of sin. We have firsthand experience of the insidious process by which sin reproduces itself. Our own involvement in sin has taught us that hatred breeds hatred, lying breeds lying, cheating breeds cheating, and fear of these sins breeds fear of these sins. Historical skepticism has become a philosophy of life among many good people who believe that individuals can be moral but communities cannot.

Moral fear can also originate, paradoxically, from grace. By "grace" I mean the very experiences of faith and charity that we cannot produce in ourselves but that arrive soon after we invite them. If one were to ask for the grace to see what is truly valuable and truly worthless in, say, one's church, the revelation may indeed be given. Then one has purchased a peck of trouble. Jeremiah and Jonah did not relish seeing the truth. Nor did they relish the power to speak it. Jeremiah could not contain his heart's fire, and Jonah could not escape being swallowed up by the Lord's whale and spit upon the beach of Nineveh.

Hope may be *for* the future, but it is not exactly *about* the future. It is about the present capacities of the human soul to make a better future. Our capacities are ambiguous to us. We do not know whether our fears spring from sin or from grace. We cannot sort out mixed motives before we must act. Our very desires are permanently suspect.

Then we recall love, and hope blossoms. This is true of human love, but it is preeminently true of divine love. Think of the times when you let yourself notice your love for God despite all your griefs. The very power of love in your own heart can bring an assurance that this power can be tapped in others whose sin is just as much rooted in fear as your own. That is, your own familiarity with moral fear and its evaporation under the rays of love will render your desire for God's Reign confident and strong.

Again, a wise mentor in this situation will not rely on the normal supports to hope (whereas an unwise mentor may simply offer deeper levels of fellow-feeling). It is not entirely unbeneficial for a retreatant to realize that one cannot give oneself hope. Ultimately we cannot even give hope to each other. Ordinarily, of course, we can and should encourage one another, but when a retreatant must make a basic commitment about his or her life, it is an extremely worthwhile experience to ask God to take away fear, to wait, and then to experience the gift of assurance and confident desire as direct gifts from God pouring down like sunshine and burning off the clouds of fear.

## 7. THE DECISION: REALIZING ONE'S CONVERSION

The nearer a retreatant approaches a decision, the less directive a mentor should become. There is no "method" a mentor can point to for making a good decision other than the imagining, noticing, meditating, contemplating, and deliberating of a person in love. This is between the retreatant and God.

Yet I do not mean to imply that decision making is so shrouded in mystery that we cannot understand anything about it. On the contrary, the mentor ought to have as clear an understanding as possible of what the retreatant is doing by making a basic decision. This understanding will enable the mentor to know when to stay out of the way and when to intervene with a remark or a caution.

From a practical standpoint, basic decisions—to resign from a job, to join a religious community, to speak out against injustice—facilitate a thousand instrumental decisions about how to live out that basic decision. Indeed, we experience the need for a basic decision when the instrumental decisions become too costly or too diverse to handle every day. So, for example, economic pressures on a married couple with four children may prompt them to reexamine their assumption that they want a fifth. Basic decisions facilitate instrumental decisions by giving them a criterion: both a religious sister and a married woman choose a job with their state of life in mind; their choice of a state of life gives a standard by which they assess which occupation to engage in.

Basic decisions also give a scale of values against which to measure life's sacrifices. More often than not, our decisions are between two good options, not between good and evil. The difficulty lies in weighing two values. When a person's affective or religious orientation in life gives them their highest value, he or she more easily sacrifices social or physical values, as we might see in a person shouldering heavy burdens as "the price of a higher choice."

I have said that a decision is a link between spirit and history. Another way of saying the same thing is this: A decision realizes one's conversion; that is, it makes one's conversion in the order of spirit a reality in the order of history.

A conversion, after all, is first of all a change of heart. It is not yet action. It ought eventually to issue in action, but until it does, it remains unspecified. Its concrete ramifications remain unknown. And when it does show in action, the shifts in values that even the converted person cannot fully name become obvious for many to name. A wise mentor will honor the profundity of a conversion in an individual but will remind the individual that there are yet many unnoticed shifts in his or her relationships that will be affected.

Of course, a retreatant may be passionately thirsting for historical change, without suspecting how even love in the heart can be biased. A genuine conversion is not only affective, it is also moral and intellectual—that is, it integrates one's heart and guts with one's mind. It does so by tempering passion with an intelligent assessment of which actions will produce the most good for the most people in the long run.

The mentor should therefore listen for a harmony between the retreatant's heart and the historical situation she or he is in. One way to detect this harmony is to imagine not this individual person in this isolated situation but rather the living God bringing about the Kingdom—working by Word and Spirit in this individual. In other words, the mentor should keep the full context of the retreat decision in mind.

Finally, the wise mentor ought to be ready to witness a rather strange phenomenon: *Many people cannot say exactly when they made the basic decision that governs their lives.* Whether in a retreat situation or not, people deliberating about a basic decision seem to one day wake up and discover that the decision has been made. There was no "picking" among options. They remember weighing many sides of various options; they recall waiting upon God for the wisdom to see and the power to act. Then, without fanfare, they simply discover that they cannot do otherwise than take this path and not that one. It is as if the decision was made *in* them more than *by* them.

What is going on here? Recall what we said in section 4 about the criterion for a value judgment. Feelings give indications of possible value, but value judgments depend on the absence of relevant questions of value. The criterion is the discovery of something missing in experience, namely, nagging questions and feelings. We appreciate something when all depreciating considerations fall away and our affectivity, mind, and body resonate in an integral response to beauty, worth, goodness. It is what we ordinarily call a peaceful conscience.

In a healthy basic decision, the decision to do what love reveals actually comes prior to knowing which option it entails. The decision is a blank check waiting to be filled out. There follows the deliberation about which of several options love's eye approves, all the while being ready to embrace any one of them. Gradually, we rest our gaze on one option and wait to see if relevant questions or uneasy feelings arise. When none do, we have discovered God's heart's desire.

Here is where experience and personal familiarity with God enable the mentor to distinguish between a solid and a shaky decision in a retreatant. If the retreatant does not begin the deliberation process with a Yes to what love will reveal, there is a need to ask God for the faith, charity, and hope that can follow through on options that seem frightful. Ignatius Loyola insisted on an "indifference" to the outcome before weighing the merits of the various options. It is indeed a grace; we cannot make ourselves "indifferent" in this sense by stoic determination. We must ask God for a readiness to pour our passion into what love will discover.

As the deliberation process develops, the absence of relevant questions in the retreatant does not mean that no relevant questions can still be asked. A mature retreatant knows this and is ready to let the option stand the test of time for a while. So the mentor might ask, "Have you considered such-and-such?" in order to let the retreatant experience possibly relevant questions. A mentor should not suddenly intervene with parentlike statements such as "I don't think this is a good decision." Such a remark tells the retreatant, in effect, that he or she is not really taking responsibility for a decision but rather guessing what the mentor wants. The precept for a mentor during a time of a retreatant's deliberation is *Raise relevant questions but let the retreatant's love reveal values.*

## 8. THE DECISION: A COLLABORATIVE ACTION

Existentialists have provided philosophy and theology with profound insight into individual responsibility. Similarly, social and historical philosophers have illuminated our common responsibility for the social order. But even the best of them talk within a strictly moral framework without dealing with the human need for faith, charity, and hope. They cannot find a common ground in faith that will resolve the differences between their many moral pronouncements.

They can make moral pronouncements on charity to the neighbor, but they cannot make people act accordingly. And their statements often have the effect of diminishing rather than expanding hope for the human race. They do not acknowledge the religious / affective dynamic of the human soul that leads people to worship God and effectively sacrifice self for the neighbor.

The problem with the atheism of contemporary existentialist and social philosophies is that by default of mentioning a living God, they teach that we are utterly alone in our human authenticity and choice, taking responsibility into our hands like solitary individuals subject to the unreasonable vicissitudes of history and plain dumb luck.

There are certainly clues in the experience of any reflective adult that suggest we are not alone in our decision but that our decision is essentially a collaborative one. I say this not so much to convince any reader that God gives prevenient and cooperative grace (although a phenomenal number of Christians act as though their decisions are sheerly solitary). Rather, my intention is to explain how these graces are experienced so that we might more easily notice the finger of God in our lives.

The easiest way to notice God's role in our decision making is to imagine trying to make a decision without the inner Word and outer Word. Without the inner Word, without God as Spirit in consciousness, we would be imprisoned by our moral relativism, impotence, and fear. Without the love of God in our hearts, we would lack the wisdom that sees values in the concrete. Even if we had the wisdom, we would lack the power to carry out our love of neighbor. Even with the wisdom and the power, we would lack the assurance that dialectical praxis done in love truly brings about God's Reign in history.

Likewise, without the outer Word of Christ Jesus in our history, we would lack the visible model of what perfect love looks like. We would lack the camaraderie with Christ and Christians that emboldens us to let our love go all the way.

We would lack the incarnate, historical promise of God that no death is ultimate. We would indeed be utterly alone, as many existentialists say we are.

## 9. INTEGRATING THE CHOICE
## INTO ONE'S LIFE

As I mentioned in the previous chapter, after the retreatant makes a basic decision, there is a second phase for contemplation, for meditation, and for noticing. Before the decision was made the effort was mainly on assessing one's existing relationships and the shifts in relationships that would result from this or that basic decision. But after such a basic decision there remains the task of integrating the decision into one's total life. Let us look again briefly at what this entails.

*Contemplation.* Here the retreatant aims to integrate the decision into his or her total worldview. The main object of contemplation here is not "God" but "God's Dream"—the concrete historical situation one loves, not alone but with the very love of God flooding over from the heart. One contemplates the new set of relationships that the decision has created—the new self one becomes, the more intimate God, the more beloved earth.

It is very important to spend time here. On the one hand, this contemplative moment may surface further questions that went unnoticed, leading the retreatant perhaps to alter the basic decision somewhat. On the other hand, contemplation may deepen one's identity as a collaborator with God, as a temple of God and a living Word of God. It is this new sense of identity that will help carry a person through the leaner days to come.

In most cases God leads us to make a basic decision without our knowing exactly how we are supposed to carry it out. In our example of John, the store manager (chapter 7), he knew that he was going to provide benefits for part-time employees, even against the advice of fellow managers, but had yet to work out how. Indeed, are there any basic decisions in the Bible where a person is given the map ahead of time? A mentor may suggest any of the many calls in Scripture as apt material for this contemplation of how God invites us to walk forward in great trust.

Contemplation, therefore, helps us put our trust in God, that God will provide not only the heart resources we will need at the crises that lay ahead but also the historical resources of a helping hand along the way. God comes, after all, as Spirit and Word—in heart and in history—and God is faithful.

In the *Spiritual Exercises* of Ignatius the retreatant is invited to spend the Third Week walking with the suffering Christ or, what is more accurate, allowing the suffering Christ to walk with him or her. Contemplation here means that the retreatant make a real assent to the reality that Christ does suffer with us as we face any painful costs of a decision. The Spirit, who is God, really does join our spirit, sharing the sufferings of Christ so as to share his glory (Rom 8:16–17).

And in the Fourth Week the retreatant is invited to share in the joy of the Spirit and of Christ. Again, this contemplation cannot happen without the real assent to the truth that God's joy can be our own. It is perhaps ironic that retreatants find it much more demanding on their faith to believe they can share in the joy of God than to share in the sufferings of God. Mentors find that the grace of the Fourth Week can be especially elusive, confused as it often is with mere joy that the retreat is over, or that Jesus' suffering is over. Jesus' joy, the joy of the Spirit, is that the long-promised salvation has finally arrived for Jerusalem and for the world.

*Meditation.* In the chapter on meditation we noted that meditation helps to integrate the decision into one's life by gathering the requisite insights needed to live out the decision. For example, a mother may decide to be much more strict with her daughter who is on drugs. How she will go about doing that is a matter of meditation, because any change in one relationship usually implies a change in many other relationships. There are her other children to consider, the responsibility of her husband, the opinions of well-meaning friends, to name a few.

But besides these practical and interpersonal aspects of her decision, there is the religious aspect. She needs to understand her actions as modeled on the action of God as revealed in Christ. It will help, therefore, if she meditates on how Christ dealt with his intransigent disciples and relatives, and especially on his own grieving care for the people he loved.

One of the most helpful exercises in taking on a Christian identity is to read the Gospels with this question in mind: What was going on in Jesus' heart that prompted him to say or do this? Granted, the answer is a matter of speculation, and one is not trying to come up with a biographical account of Jesus' thoughts, but we grow in our knowledge and love of our dearest friends by the same kind of speculative wonder about their hearts—that is, we grow in familiarity with another precisely by this kind of speculation. It will never give us certitude about what Jesus actually was thinking, but it can give us a growing familiarity with the values Jesus espoused in his daily life.

During a time of retreat, while the practical aspects of a basic decision may be considered, it is usually better to concentrate on the religious meanings and ramifications of the decision. The practical aspects, after all, are still somewhat hidden to the retreatant, while the religious aspects can easily be meditated upon at this time.

*Noticing.* Finally, to complete the "Circle of Praxis" we sketched out in chapter 2, the retreatant can expect to notice the world in a quite different manner. One's attention is transformed by love—a love determined to carry out a decision, a love shrewd as a serpent, a love that takes heaven by storm.

If the retreatant has been sequestered during the body of the retreat, it is wise to let this person return to the shopping malls, the parks, the rundown areas of town in order to see with different eyes what used to hold very different meanings. It can help immensely to talk explicitly of faith, charity, and hope—and their opposites: moral relativism, frigidity, and fear—and to see the world in these terms. It can help also to talk explicitly of one's imaginal theology of history as one rides a bus or visits a friend in the hospital. The retreatant's basic decision may have been a powerful grace from God, but without the intellectual and imaginal reenvisioning of the world, the complete reintegration of one's relationships around the basic decision will not occur. The very meaning of a *basic* decision is that it affects all the details of one's life.

These last three phases of a retreat—the contemplation, meditation, and noticing that follow a basic decision—ought to begin to some degree before the retreat is formally ended. But they should be the ordinary way of praying for a good long time after the retreat. There is a temptation to slide back into feeling that God is distant and that one needs some moral reform to get back into God's good graces. This is nothing but forgetfulness of the good news that we are already reconciled with God, not by our actions but by God's kind mercy. There is needed rather the faith that the actions we perform in love constitute our union with the God who loves the world.

The mentor, therefore, should be vigilant. Old pious habits in the retreatant may creep in and leave the person trying to reach God or to draw some moral about how to be a better person. Making progress in the spiritual life is certainly a value, but it can be a red herring when a person needs to make the many adjustments demanded by a basic decision.

Furthermore, the mentor should not automatically terminate the relationship with the retreatant once the formal retreat time has ended. The retreatant still needs a soul friend to walk with in order to grow accustomed to this new active union with God. Ideally there would be some spiritual support group one can join. In any case, the topic of maintaining what has been gained must be dealt with explicitly between the retreatant and the mentor.

Finally, need it be said that the mentor has collaborated in a basic decision and that therefore he or she should spend time alone contemplating, meditating, and noticing how God's Dream has been realized in this room, around this table, with this soul friend? It is a humbling privilege to walk with someone welcoming the grace of decision. In the real history that cannot be written, these moments are the turning points of world process. The mentor does well to remember: "It is God, for his own loving purpose, who puts both the will and the action into you . . . and you will shine in the world like bright stars because you are offering it the word of life" (Phil 2:13, 16).

# APPENDIX

---

# Psychoanalysis, Counseling, Spiritual Mentoring

I have talked about several different functions that a spiritual mentor must perform, and some of these overlap the functions of psychoanalysts and counselors. It may help if I summarize and schematize the relationships among these various services.

Strictly speaking, psychoanalysis is just that—analysis. It is not therapy. Its aim is to understand what one is feeling, about what, and why. It does not give counsel about what to do. Indeed, the strict Freudian psychoanalysts seem to believe that analysis is all one needs, as if understanding one's emotions automatically reveals what to do about them. But understanding one's emotions does not automatically evaluate their direction—as people who have spent years "in analysis" often attest. There is the further work of evaluating and prioritizing one's felt desires.

Counseling provides a person with advice—about the long-range worth of various options if not outright advice about what to do. It provides "counsel." It certainly goes beyond mere psychoanalysis, but it too works within its own limited framework. It goes beyond the cognitive need to understand our desires and fears to the moral need to evaluate them. Yet, as we saw, the moral order is itself ultimately limited by one's personal brand of moral relativism, impotence, and fear. This means that no matter how sound the advice coming in, a person does not necessarily experience conviction about one option over another, particularly when both options seem good. He or she is caught in moral relativism. Furthermore, even when one option seems best, it does not necessarily follow that a person has the courage to carry it out, particularly when lingering resentments make it almost impossible to deal charitably with an old enemy. And, last, the eye of faith and the guts of charity do not by themselves eliminate the fear that even our best efforts will come to naught. It is one thing to hear a counselor's words of hope and quite another to experience the gift of hope in the heart.

The chief function of a spiritual mentor (whether it be in a formal relation called as such or merely part of a friendship) is to *monitor the experiences of faith, charity, and hope in the retreatant.* This involves asking apposite questions, providing necessary information, suggesting materials for meditation, and above all, keeping the context of the choice the full Reign of God in history. The mentor actually does less analyzing than the analyst and less counseling than the counselor because his or her role is to assist a person in making a truly free choice—a choice without compulsion, a choice freed from addiction, a choice the mentor cannot make for the person. In this sense a mentor performs mainly the negative function of watching to see that the retreatant is not getting into trouble because of a narrow worldview or because of excessive clinging to personal security or to a sense of belonging to some community.

I do not mean to imply that the cognitive, moral, and religious functions need to be separated—only distinguished. Just as a chemist needs to understand the physics on which chemistry depends, and the biology that chemistry underpins, so the psychoanalyst, counselor, and spiritual mentor do well to understand where their specialties fit into the hierarchy of skilled help.

Typically psychoanalysts look down on counselors, and yet professional counselors help as many people in their clinical work as the analysts do—reportedly more quickly and a lot more cheaply. Likewise, both psychoanalysts and counselors typically disparage taking seriously a client's relationship to God. And yet the evidence of Alcoholics Anonymous and a number of other recent movements in faith healing demonstrates an effectiveness beyond what scientists can explain. Thus, although spiritual mentors need to know when to keep their hands off problems that psychoanalysts or counselors can handle better, the latter need to know when to refer a client to a trained spiritual mentor.

What is even more serious, psychoanalysts typically avoid moral and spiritual issues, skipping from mere understanding of the past to mere understanding of a possible future, without dealing explicitly with the moral and spiritual / religious experiences that occur in a client in any case. A similar criticism can be leveled against many counselors. Typically they will seek the requisite understanding and go on to questions of value, but they fail to talk about the experiences of faith, charity, and hope that constitute the core of spiritual experience. People who take their spiritual experiences seriously know very well that being in love reveals values, gives courage, and instills hope in ways beyond what mere ethical reflection, let alone mere psychological acumen, can give. Yet taking spiritual experiences seriously is one thing and being able to talk articulately about what effect they have on a decision is another.

So spiritual mentoring is not some fluffy extra enjoyed by people who have the leisure to talk religion together. It is a basic human need that stems from the simple facts that all people experience faith, charity, and hope and that these experiences have an impact on how they live.

Here is a sketch of the functions a spiritual mentor would likely address. I presume that some relatively easy psychoanalysis and counseling are part of spiritual mentoring, not as its goal but as preliminary to its goal of helping a person make a decision impelled by love of God and neighbor. Also, although these notes summarize much of what I have said above, they hardly exhaust the relevant functions. The sketch needs filling out, in other words, by a mentor's own wisdom and experience.

| FUNCTION | QUESTIONS | LIMITS |
|---|---|---|
| Psychoanalysis (cognitive) | What do you desire?<br><br>What feeling are you having?<br><br>What is the object of that feeling?<br><br>Are some of these feelings or their objects masking more essential feelings or objects? | Unable to criticize feelings, to pose the question of ethics, morality, objective right and wrong.<br><br>Unable to recognize and understand the experiences of faith, charity, and hope. |
| Counseling (moral) | What is the objectively best thing to do in this situation?<br><br>Which feelings should you trust?<br><br>What ethical voices do you hear—from the situation, from cultural mores, from your belief system?<br><br>Are any "shoulds" arising from your superego? | Moral relativism<br><br>Moral frigidity<br><br>Moral fear<br><br>Unable to recognize and understand the experiences of faith, charity, and hope. |

| FUNCTION | QUESTIONS | LIMITS |
|---|---|---|
| Spiritual Mentoring (religious / affective)<br><br>(spiritual companion, soul friend, spiritual director) | What is God calling you to?<br><br>Are you letting love inspire your deliberation?<br><br>What pulls and counterpulls do you experience? Which come from God and which do not?<br><br>What imaginal theology of history does your behavior reveal?<br><br>What wisdom and realizations (faith) does your love give you?<br><br>What power and courage (charity) does your love give you?<br><br>What assurance and confidence (hope) does your love give you? | No certitude available.<br><br>No autonomous "conviction" available. |

It is my fond hope that spiritual mentoring will be respected by the helping professions, that psychoanalysts, counselors, and social workers will be able to recognize when people have religious or transcendent dimensions to their struggles and will, far from ignoring them, refer them to trained spiritual mentors. Conversely, mentors must be trained in at least enough psychology to be able to deal with low-level psychological problems and to know when to refer a person to a psychologist or counselor. To achieve this co-operation, however, mentor training will have to meet established standards. There will have to be training programs, review processes, certifications, financing, and a body of literature that explores guided spiritual discretion in a self-critical and accountable fashion.

In the United States, where church and state issues are sharply separated, the issue of payments for spiritual mentoring—odious as it sounds—must be dealt with. The labor deserves the wages. Not to pay spiritual mentors means that few people will be able to consider the work as a profession and few, therefore, will receive the services.

Credentialing trained spiritual mentors is another delicate area. No doubt many women and men have been giving fine spiritual guidance without any credentials. But there are as many ill-prepared people offering "spiritual guidance" but giving mere techniques or acting in a parental role or offering pious answers to what are psychological or even medical problems. While little can be done about the well-meaning zealot who wants to hang out a shingle offering spiritual advice, at least a national credentialing service could be created by an interdenominational consortium of the schools and seminaries that offer training in spiritual mentoring. That credentialing would be a minimal guarantee for those aware of the dangers of mere pious opinions that the mentor has undergone training, supervision, and testing.

As I read over what I have written, I find that many of my remarks are merely pointers to areas that need to be developed further. On the one hand, I do not feel I have all the answers, while on the other, I did not want to ignore some rather complex issues simply because they are complex. My chief aim has been to discuss the theological dimensions of spiritual mentoring and the connections spirituality has to psychology and ethics. If it leaves no other impression than the great need for an educated mentor, I would be happy. But I hope it also has clarified some of your own questions about giving or receiving spiritual mentoring.

# Notes

## INTRODUCTION

[1]There are a number of translations available, all with consistent paragraph numbers. See Louis Puhl, trans., *The Spiritual Exercises of St. Ignatius* (Chicago: Loyola Univ. Press, 1951), par. 21. For another excellent approach to Ignatius' *Exercises* see Gilles Cusson, *Biblical Theology and the Spiritual Exercises: A Method Towards a Personal Experience of God as Accomplishing within Us His Plan of Salvation*, trans. M. Roduit and G. Ganss (St. Louis: Institute of Jesuit Sources, 1988).

[2]See my *Lonergan and Spirituality* (Chicago: Loyola Univ. Press, 1985) for how attention to method in philosophy has profound ramifications for spirituality studies.

[3]An old Celtic saying: "Anyone without a soul friend is a body without a head." See Paul Begheyn, "Traditions of Spiritual Guidance," *The Way* 29 (June 1989): 156, 165.

## 1. RETREAT: REALIZING OUR BAPTISM

[1]George Aschenbrenner, S.J., "Consciousness Examen," *Review for Religious* 31 (1972): 14–21.

## 2. SPIRITUAL PRAXIS

[1]*Spiritual Exercises*, pars. 169–89.

[2]This is the original title of what a later editor entitled "Rules for Discernment of Spirits"—a term Ignatius used very seldom. He preferred the term *conoscere*, which means to grow familiar with someone, to recognize them by their style. A better title for his

rules might be "Guidelines for Becoming Familiar with Our Inner Experiences."

[3]"[During the Spanish Civil War], hundreds of thousands of young people and adults in the dominant elite which had won the civil war not only did the [*Spiritual Exercises* of Saint Ignatius], but assiduously practiced the 'particular examination' of the individual cogito. But we do not know of a single case of anyone who discovered the depths of falsehood in his own self-awareness by means of this practice. Not one of these Christians who followed the Exercises discovered the tremendous contradiction (to Christianity) in prisons still full of ideological prisoners and a proletariat bitterly exploited and silenced by ferocious political repression. This is natural: a monologue with one's own self-awareness is incapable of realizing its own radically false ideology." Fernando Urbina, "On Spirit and History," in C. Floristan and C. Duquoc, eds., *Discernment of Spirit and Spirits* (New York: Seabury / Crossroad, 1979), 120–21.

[4]The Myers-Briggs analysis uses a forced-choice test drawn from the writings of Carl Jung to categorize a person's decision-making style along four continua: Intravert or Extravert; Sensate or Intuitive; Feeling or Thinking; Judging or Perceiving. The Enneagram is an arcane pathology (until recently it has been an entirely oral tradition) of nine basic but relatively unnoticed compulsions. The object is to discover which compulsion is your own. Personally, I have found the Enneagram more useful than the Myers-Briggs types in maintaining the dialectical attitude toward the human spirit. See, for example, Helen Palmer, *The Enneagram: Understanding Yourself and the Others in Your Life* (San Francisco: Harper & Row, 1988). Compare with Isabel Briggs Myers, *Gifts Differing* (Palo Alto, CA: Consulting Psychologists Press, 1980), and David Keirsey, *Please Understand Me* (Del Mar, CA: Promethean Books, 1978).

## 3. OUR PRIMARY RELATIONSHIP: GOD

[1]For the ideas that the question of God belongs to human nature, and that the response of God is through an inner and an outer Word, see Bernard Lonergan, *Method in Theology* (New York: Herder & Herder, 1972), 101–15.

[2]"Ordinarily the experience of the mystery of love and awe is not objectified. It remains within subjectivity as a vector, an undertow, a fateful call to a dreaded holiness" (ibid., 113).

[3]Ibid., 112–15.

[4]Here I am following Benedict Viviano, *The Kingdom of God in History* (Wilmington, DE: Michael Glazier, 1988), chaps. 1 and 2.

## 4. THE IMAGE OF HISTORY

[1]*Insight* (New York: Philosophical Library, 1970). For a compendious account, see p. 607. For a more thoroughgoing analysis, see chaps. 2, 4, 6.5, 14.4, 15.7, and 17.

[2]For this study of the role of the Holy Spirit in the four Gospels I have relied on George Montague, *The Holy Spirit: Growth of a Biblical Tradition* (New York: Paulist Press, 1976).

[3]New York: Image / Doubleday, 1958. See esp. book 14, chaps. 26–28 and pp. 306, 310, 322, 392.

[4]Ignatius of Loyola, *The Spiritual Exercises,* ed. and trans. Louis Puhl (Westminster, MD: The Newman Press, 1959), pars. 136–48 (pp. 60–63). The idea that good and evil spirits take three mutually opposing steps in drawing our hearts toward God or evil is not original with Ignatius. Werner (d. 1126), abbot of St. Blase of the Black Forest, represented Satan as drawing us first to riches, then to pride, and finally to nonsuffering. Christ, in contrast, draws us to poverty, then to humility, and finally to the patience that suffers evil. See his "De duobus Dominus et duabus civitatibus et diversis aliis rebus" in *Los Orígenes de los Ejercicios Espiritualis de S. Ignacio de Loyola,* ed. P. Arturo Codina (Barcelona: Biblioteca Balmes, 1926), 287–89, or Migne, P.L. 157, 1144–46. Ignatius' version ends with the more positively practical "and to all other virtues." It seems likely that Werner's analysis predated the more famous *Steps of Humility* that Bernard of Clairvaux wrote around the year Werner died, but that both were developments of Benedict's twelve grades of humility. See Bernard of Clairvaux, *The Steps of Humility,* trans. and ed. George B. Burch (Cambridge, MA: Harvard Univ. Press, 1940), 95, 117.

## 5. THE PRAXIS OF NOTICING

[1]For a helpful Jungian analysis of the effect of "mood" on perception, see Robert A. Johnson, *He: Understanding Masculine Psy-*

*chology* (New York: Harper & Row / Perennial Library, 1974), 35−45.


## 6. THE PRAXIS OF MEDITATION

[1]See Frederick E. Crowe, *Theology of the Christian Word* (New York: Paulist Press, 1978). He notes in particular the thematization of the Word of God as "truth" in the struggles that preceded the creedal formulas of Nicaea and Chalcedon. He also discusses the view that history itself is God's "word"—its clear statement in Aquinas, its expansion in de Caussade and Pannenberg, and its implications for today.

[2]For early instances of codification see Jos 1:8 and Ps 1:2. For early instances of chronicles, see Wisdom 10–19 and Sirach 44–49.

[3]Early Christian thought regarding history is a complex issue. For more on the nuances, see L. G. Patterson, *God and History in Early Christian Thought: A Study of Themes from Justin Martyr to Gregory the Great* (London: Adam & Charles Black, 1966), esp. chaps. 1 and 2.

[4]See E. von Severus and A. Solignac, "Meditation," *Dictionnaire de Spiritualité,* 10, ed. M. Viller et al. (Paris: Bauchesne, 1980).

[5]"He seemed like one grieved because he had not been martyred." Robert Gregg, trans., *Athanasius: The Life of Antony and the Letter to Marcellinus* (New York: Paulist Press, 1980), 66 (pars. 46, 47).

[6]Letters 1, 77. Cited by von Severus and Solignac in "Meditation," 909.

[7]"Is not the pseudo-Dionysius the Areopagite, the inspirer of so many medieval mystics, a Platonizing philosopher to the very extent that he is a mystic? And did not his distant emulators of the thirteenth and fourteenth centuries, Eckhart, Tauler, Suso, Ruysbroeck, and their fellows, insert their most intimate experiences into the framework of a Plotinian scholasticism? Unquestionably." Joseph Marechal, *Studies in the Psychology of the Mystics,* trans. A. Thorold (Albany, NY: Magi Books, 1964), 155. For a brief overview of the philosophical roots of Christian spirituality, see the articles under that title in Cheslyn Jones et al., eds., *The Study of Spirituality* (New York: Oxford Univ. Press, 1986).

[8]See J. M. Lozano, "Eremitism," in *The Encyclopedia of Religion,* 5, ed. Mircea Eliade (New York: Macmillan Publishing, 1987), 137–46.

[9]God would be known more for engaging human history than for merely watching it from afar. Spirituality would be only partly creation centered; it would also be healing centered. Our relationship to God would be conceived as being worked out in the dialectical struggle of biased human hearts in a biased history but redeemed by the historical work of Jesus and the ongoing inner work of God as Spirit.

[10]I take Colossians to be the last letter Paul had direct connection with, even though he may not have composed it himself. Ephesians seems to be a disciple's balanced recap of Paul's theology, written perhaps with Colossians as a model but with much less the concern for local problems that characterizes Paul's letters.

[11]This issue has been explored by Jürgen Moltmann in his *Trinity and the Kingdom* (San Francisco: Harper & Row, 1981).

[12]W. Abbott, ed., "Gaudium et Spes" (Pastoral Constitution on the Church in the Modern World), *The Documents of Vatican II* (New York: Herder & Herder, 1966), par. 1 (p. 199).

[13]For example, in 1947 Pius XII insisted that meditation and spiritual exercise ought to have "practical results." His list represents the spirituality of the time: (1) subject the senses to reason illumined by faith; (2) cleanse the heart, growing more like Christ from whom to draw inspiration and strength; (3) "produce good fruit, to perform individual duties faithfully, to give themselves eagerly to the regular practice of their religion and the energetic exercise of virtue." *"Mediator Dei"* in *The Papal Encyclicals,* 4, ed. C. Carlen (Wilmington, NC: McGrath Publishing, 1981), par. 33 (pp. 125–26).

[14]See Acts 10:9–34; 13:16–41; 14:15–17; 17:22–31.

[15]Bernard Lonergan praises the proposal of Gibson Winter's *Elements for a Social Ethic* (New York: Macmillan, 1966): "Between social science and social policy he inserts social ethics." See "The Example of Gibson Winter" (1970) in *A Second Collection: Papers by Bernard Lonergan, S.J.,* ed. W. F. J. Ryan and B. J. Tyrrell (London: Darton, Longman Todd, 1974).

## 7. THE PRAXIS OF CONTEMPLATION

[1] Perhaps the culmination of the ascensional contemplation trend can be seen in Joachim of Fiore, whose "Age of the Holy Spirit," beginning in 1260, would be an age of love and freedom, without pope or sacrament, in an *ecclesia contemplativa.* Aquinas may well have influenced the more action-oriented approach of the Jesuits ("contemplation in action"). For an introductory account of these issues, see "Plotinus," "Augustine," "Joachim of Fiore," and "The Dominicans" (by Anthony Meridith, Andrew Louth, Marjorie Reeves, and Simon Tugwell, resp.) in *The Study of Spirituality,* ed. C. Jones et al. (New York: Oxford Univ. Press, 1986), 96–99; 134–45; 292–93; 296–99.

[2] J. Neville Ward, "Contemplation," in *The Westminster Dictionary of Christian Spirituality,* ed. G. Wakefield (Philadelphia: Westminster Press, 1983), 95–96. J. Aumann, "Contemplation," in *New Catholic Encyclopedia* (Washington, D.C.: Catholic University of America, 1967).

[3] Basil the Great (d. 379) taught that the Holy Spirit comes to people particularly in the liturgy, not merely to teach them but to give them the highest possible share in God's being: "Spirit-bearing souls, illumined by Him, finally become spiritual themselves, and their grace is sent forth to others. From this comes knowledge of the future, understanding of mysteries, apprehension of hidden things, distribution of wonderful gifts, heavenly citizenship, a place in the choir of angels, endless joy in the presence of God, becoming like God, and, the highest of all desires, becoming God." David Anderson, ed., *St. Basil the Great: On the Holy Spirit* (Crestwood, NY: St. Vladimir's Seminary Press, 1980), 44 (chap. 9, par. 23).

[4] John Henry Newman, *An Essay in Aid of a Grammar of Assent* (Oxford: Clarendon Press, 1985).

[5] For this and other quotations in this section see ibid., 57–64.

[6] "The person who gives . . . the order of contemplating ought to faithfully narrate the history, . . . running through the chief points with a brief summary statement. This is because the person who contemplates, by taking the true foundation of the history . . . derives greater spiritual relish and profit than if the giver of the Exercises had discoursed at great length and dilated upon the

meaning of the history. For it is not much knowledge that fills and satisfies the soul, but the inward sense and taste of things." *Spiritual Exercises of Saint Ignatius* no. 2.

[7]See F. E. Crowe, "School Without Graduates: The Ignatian Spiritual Exercises," the appendix to his *Old Things and New: A Strategy for Education* (Atlanta: Scholars Press, 1985), 157–73.

[8]See Hannah Arendt, *Willing*, vol. 2 of *The Life of the Mind* (New York: Harcourt Brace Jovanovich, 1978), 123–24.

## 8. THE PRAXIS OF DELIBERATION

[1]See Karl Lowith, *Meaning in History*, chap. 3, "Hegel" (Chicago: Univ. of Chicago Press, 1949), 52–59, in which history is dominated by a suprahuman Spirit that belittles human choice. Compare with his chap. 9, "Augustine," 160–73, in which, it seems to me, choice represents spirit without history.

[2]According to Conrad Baars, in his *Feeling and Healing Your Emotions* (Plainfield, NJ: Logos International, 1979), 14–26, these are the six basic kinds of human emotions.

[3]Originally "Conscience and Superego: A Key Distinction," *Theological Studies* 32, 1 (March 1971): 30–47. Reprinted in J. Heaney, ed., *Psyche and Spirit* (New York: Paulist Press, 1973), 33–55.

[4]This is evident from his "Rules for Discernment" nos. 314, 315, 329. See L. Puhl, trans. and ed., *The Spiritual Exercise of St. Ignatius* (Chicago: Loyola Univ. Press, 1951), 141, 157.

[5]The Christian principle that the will is not free without grace is rooted in this experience. It means we cannot effectively choose what we know is right without the gift of a *desire*—the experience of a received movement in consciousness to do what we know is good. The heresy of liberalism is the counterposition, "I can do whatever I want, as long as no one gets hurt." Christian reflection on experience reminds us that we are *unable* to do whatever we want, regardless of whether or not anyone gets hurt. See Peter Kaufman, *Augustinian Piety and Catholic Reform* (Macon, GA: Mercer Univ. Press, 1982), chap 1: "Augustine's Pursuit of Righteousness and the Question of Church Reform," 5–28.

# Index

Abraham (biblical figure), 70, 74
Adam (biblical figure), 70
Afterlife, 51, 58
Agnosticism, 22
Alcoholics Anonymous, 159, 179
Antony, Saint, 106
Apostles, 38, 69, 71; Acts of, 70, 115; ordination of, 71. *See also* Disciples of Christ
Appreciation, in contemplation, 130–33, 141, 143, 145
Aquinas, Saint Thomas, 53, 125, 145, 188n.1, 190n.1
Arendt, Hannah, 191n.8
Aristotelianism, 66, 105
Aristotle, 105, 108, 145
Art, 35, 37
Ascensional meditation/contemplation, 108–9, 143–44, 190n.1
Asceticism, 106–7, 109
Aschenbrenner, S. J., 185n.1(ch.1)
Assent, real, 133–42, 159, 173; dynamics of, 139–42; essence of, 136–39; vs. notional assent, 134–36, 142
Assessment of relationships, 8–9, 12, 85, 86–87, 100–1, 119, 121–22, 142–43, 149, 172
Athanasius, Saint, 106, 188n.5
Augustine, Saint, 12, 51, 57, 75–76, 77, 106, 108, 146, 148–49,

158; *City of God*, 76; and contemplation, 125, 126; *On the Christian Combat*, 75
Aumann, J., 190n.2
Authority: hierarchical, 110–11, 113; personal, 149, 154; questioning of, 114

Baars, Conrad, 191n.2
Baptism, 1–3, 71
Basil the Great, Saint, 190n.3
Battle, image of, 79
Begheyn, Paul, 185n.3
Behavior, as mirror of feelings, 89
Benedict, Saint, 187n.4(ch.4)
Bergman, Ingmar, 22
Bernard of Clairvaux, Saint, 187n.4(ch.4)
Bible, 21, 73, 74, 106, 107, 109; Acts of the Apostles, 70, 115; Beatitudes, 94; how to read, 112–13; New Testament, 42, 51, 53, 104, 106, 109–10, 128, 159; Old Testament, 51, 56, 95, 106, 126, 128; purpose of reading, 9; Sermon on the Mount, 67. *See also* Biblical citations; Gospels
Biblical citations: Leviticus (**17:3**), 146; Job (**38:12, 28–29, 31, 35; 39:1**), 33–34; Job (**42:3–6**), 134; Proverbs (**16:30**), 119; Mark

(**12:30**), 120; Mark (**14:35**), 160; John (**14:12**), 40; Romans (**7:15**), 158; Romans (**8:16–17**), 173; Romans (**8:23**), 132; Romans (**14:17**), 51; Ephesians (**1:17–18**), 95–96; Philippians (**2:13, 16**), 176; Philippians (**4:5**), 164; Colossians (**1:15–20**), 41; Colossians (**1:24**), 40; Colossians (**1:27–29**), 75; 1 John (**4:11**), 39; Revelation (**21:2**), 58
Bonaventure, Saint, 107
"Born Again," 43, 109

Catholicism, 52
Celibacy, 12, 107
Certification/credentialing, of spiritual mentors, 182
Chalcedon, Council of, 188n.1
Charity, 97–98, 163, 164–65, 166, 170–71, 178, 179
Choice: as essence of retreat, 2–3; facing, 139, 150–61, 167–68; freedom of, 16–17, 178, 191n.5; making, 20, 25–26, 27, 30, *diagram*, 31, 63, 96, 97, 142–44, 168–70, 186n.4; putting into effect, 122, 143, 168, 172–76. *See also* Decisions
Christ, 55, 75–76, 107, 108, 173, 187n.4(ch.4); divine status of, 43, 110, 163; Passion of, 35, 73. *See also* Jesus of Nazareth
Christianity: authority principle in Church, 110–11, 113; early, *xvi*, 54, 70–71, 75, 163; early writings, 105–8, 110, 125; Johannine church, 69; Matthew's church, 67. *See also* Catholicism
*City of God* (Saint Augustine), 76
City of God, 51, 53, 150. *See also* Kingdom of God; Reign of God
Classical kind of insight, 64, 65, 66, 79

Classic works, 23–24
Clement, Pope (Saint Clement), 106, 108
Community, 38, 54–55, 58, 165, 166; interruptive ideal of, 81; vs. Kingdom, 49–50; preservative ideal of, 81; reconciliation with spiritual praxis, 24–26; responsibility, 81, 170; selfishness, 49, 78, 81, 102
Compassion, 44, 79
Compulsion, 27, 98, 123; enneagraphic, 186n.4
Conscience, 153–61; as arbiter of values, 153–57; defined, 155, 157; examination of, 9, 122, 123; limits of, 157–61; peaceful, 169; vs. superego, 155–56
Consciousness, 156–57; examination of, 9, 101; inner data of, 88–89, 91; noticing and questioning of, 88–89, 90–91
Consolation, 96–98, 99–102, 122
Constantine, Emperor, 51, 57
Constantinople, decrees of, *xvi*
Contemplation, 30, *diagram*, 31, 107, 120, 124, 125–46, 150; "in action," 126, 145; ascensional, 108–9, 124, 143–44, 190n.1; definitions of, 104, 111, 125–33; vs. insight, 130–31, 142; vs. meditation, 104, 125, 128, 134; prechoice and postchoice purposes of, 142–44; return phase of, 124, 143–44, 172–73, 175–76
Conversion, 3, 122, 162, 168
Counseling, 177–78, 179, 180; questions and limits of, 180
Creation, God's Word in, 34, 37–38, 41, 45
Creativity, 78, 79, 81, 82, 156–57
Crowe, Frederick E., 188n.1, 191n.7
Cusson, Gilles, 185n.1(intro)

De Caussade, Pierre, 188n.1

Decisions, decision making, 148–50, 167–72; conscience as guide to, 153–61; feelings as preliminaries to, 150–53; integration of, 172–76; as link between spirit and history, 148–50, 168; questions in, 150, 170; role of love in, 161–67, 169–70, 171

Deliberation, praxis of, 30, *diagram*, 31, 147–76; return phase, 172–76. *See also* Choice; Decisions

Desert Fathers, 75

Desolation, 96–100, 122, 131

Dialectical image, 71–73, 78–83, 158; history of, 74–78

Dialectical kind of insight, 65, 79

Dionysius the Areopagite, 188n.7

"Discerning the Will of God," 16–17

Discernment of spirits, 16–20, 21, 48, 67, 191n.4; term, 16–17, 185n.2(ch.2)

Discernment of stories, 21–22, 48

Discernment skills, 17–19

Disciples of Christ, 40, 67, 69, 72, 137, 163. *See also* Apostles

Disney, Walt, 22

Disobedience, inner, 48, 57–58

Doctrine, *xv*, 12, 33, 45; of salvation, 42; of the Trinity, 44

Dogmatism, 28


Eckhart, Johannes, 188n.7

Emotions, basic, 151, 191n.2. *See also* Feelings

Enneagram, 27, 186n.4

Eremitic life, 106–7, 109

Erikson, Erik, 64

Essenes, 107

Eusebius of Caesarea, 51

Evangelists, 73–74, 105. *See also* John; Luke; Mark; Matthew

Evil, 34–35, 74, 76, 80, 165–66,
187n.4(ch.4). *See also* Sinfulness

Examination of conscience, 9, 122, 123

Examination of consciousness, 9, 101

Existentialists, 170–71, 172


Faith, 97–98, 163–64, 165, 166, 170, 178, 179

Faith healing, 179

*Federalist, The*, 23

Feelings, 131, 133; ambiguity of, 152, 164; basic kinds of, 151, 191n.2; behavior as mirror of, 89; "being in touch" with, 151–52; vs. conscience, 155, 157; noticing of, 88–89, 96; role as preliminaries to decision, 150–53

Fiction literature, 21–22

Franciscans, 107

Freedom: of choice (will), 16–17, 178, 191n.5; spiritual, 68

Freud, Sigmund, 20

Freudian psychoanalysis, 177. *See also* Psychoanalysis

Friendship, 65

Frye, Northrop, 73

Fundamentalists, *xvi*, 77


Galileo Galilei, 64

Genetic kind of insight, 64

Glaser, John, 155–56

Gnosticism, 22

Goal images, 61

God: doctrines of, 12, 33, 44, 45; love for, 36, 38, 39, 40–42, 43, 45, 75, 81, 120, 145–46, 162–63, 166; love for, noticing, 88–89, 171; love of (for man), *xv*, 5, 13, 36, 42–43, 123; metaphors for, 32, 52; search for, 42–43; sources of knowledge of, 11, 33, 162; two processions of, 44; understanding of term, 10–12, 30, 32; views of social sciences on, 121; Who? question about, 36, 37, 41, 145; Why? question to, 34–35, 37, 39–40, 132. *See also* Kingdom of God; Reign of God; Spirit of God; Will of God; Word of God

Gospels, the, 35, 43, 73–74, 105–6, 107; of John, 40, 68–69, 74; of Luke, 70–71, 74; of Mark, 72–73, 105, 120, 160; of Matthew, 49, 67, 74; reading, 174

Grace, 80–81, 161, 166, 170, 171, 173

"Grace of office," of spiritual mentor, 164

Greece: early Church in, 67, 106–7; philosophy and cosmology, 105, 107, 109

Greed, 47, 48–49, 79, 147

Gregory of Nyssa, 106

*Guernica* (Picasso), 35

Guilt feelings, 99–100, 155, 156

Hammarskjöld, Dag, 37

Hatred, 48–49, 80, 166; inner, 39, 50

Hebrew traditions, 110; of meditation, 105

Hegel, Georg Wilhelm Friedrich, 76, 148

Hinduism, 107

History, 54–56, 78–80, 113–14, 148; God's Word in, 38–39, 41–42, 43, 44, 45, 53–56, 105, 106–7, 188n.1; imaginal theology of, 31, 60–83, 108, 175; Reign of God as force in, 54–59, 114; soul's dialectic identical to dialectic of, 75

Holy Spirit, *xvi*, 42, 107, 109–11, 190n.3; in doctrine of the Trinity, 44, 111; in the four Gospels, 67, 69, 70–71, 72, 187n.2(ch.4). *See also* Spirit of God

Hope, 98, 163, 165–67, 170–71, 178, 179

Hugh of St. Victor, 108

Ignatius of Loyola, Saint, 2, 76, 77, 96–97, 99, 100, 170; "discernment" of, 16–17, 185n.2(ch.2), 191n.4; *Spiritual Exercises, xiii, xiv,* 1, 137, 144, 173, 185n.1(intro), 187n.4(ch.4), 190n.6

Images and imagination, 60–83, 131, 137, 150; defined, 66; dialectical, 71–73, 74–83, 158; goal, 61–62; Gospel correspondence, 73; interruptive, 68–69, 74–75, 76, 77, 78, 81–82, 113, 157; preservative, 66–68, 69, 70, 74–75, 76, 77, 78, 81–82, 113, 157; process, 61–63; process, kinds of, 63, 66–74; progressive, 69–71, 72, 74–75, 76–77, 78, 81–82, 113, 157–58

Indian asceticism, 107

*Insight* (Lonergan), 63, 187n.1(ch.4)

Insights, 81, 96, 130–31, 142, 151; classical, 64, 65, 66, 79; dialectical, 65, 79; genetic, 64–65; statistical, 64, 65

Integration of relationships, 9–10, 12, 119, 121, 122–23, 142–43, 149, 172–76

Interconnectedness, 58–59

Interruptive image, 68–69, 74–75, 76, 77, 78, 81–82, 113, 157

Irenaeus, Saint, 50, 106

Irish civil war, 82

Israel, 74–75, 105; ages of, 51

Jairus (biblical figure), 92

Jeremiah (prophet), 166

Jesus of Nazareth, 41, 53, 56, 61–62, 68–69, 72–73, 107, 109–11, 147, 160; genealogy of (New Adam), 70; the human vs. the divine, 43, 111, 163; inner life of, 91–95, 174; and "Kingdom of God," 52–53; his life as Word of God, *xv, xvi,* 39, 40–41, 44, 46, 137, 171; Sermon on the Mount, 67; in the wilderness, 72. *See also* Christ

Joachim of Fiore, 76, 190n.1

Job (biblical figure), real vs. notional assent of, 134

Joel (prophet), 71

John (apostle), 70, 94, 110, 126; Gospel of, 40, 68–69, 74

John of the Cross, Saint, 108

Johnson, Robert A., 187n.1(ch.5)

Jonah (biblical figure), 166

Journey, image of, 79

Joy: experience of, 94–95, 112; of God, sharing, 173

Judgment, 123; of fact, 130, 135; of value, 90, 98, 100, 124, 130–31, 133, 135, 139, 151, 153–54, 163, 168–70

Jung, Carl, 186n.4, 187n.1(ch.5)

Kaufman, Peter, 191n.5

Keirsey, David, 186n.4

Kingdom of God (*or* of heaven), 49–53, 54, 56, 122–23; ambiguity of meanings, 50, 51; apocalyptic-eschatological vision of, 51, 54; vs. community, 49–50; inadequacy of term, 50, 52–53; sexist connotation of term, 50, 52; as unfamiliar metaphor, 50, 52

*King Lear* (Shakespeare), 21

Labels (of psychology, sociology, etc.), 27–28

Lewis, C. S., 22

"Liberation" praxis, 28–29

Liberation theology, 28, 49

*Life of Antony* (Athanasius), 106

Lonergan, Bernard, 63–64, 186n.1, 189n.15

*Lonergan and Spirituality* (Dunne), 185n.2(intro)

Love: concrete meaning of, 116–20, 128–30, 140–42, 145; for God, 36, 38, 39, 40–42, 43, 45, 75, 81, 120, 145–46, 162–63, 166; for God, noticing, 88–89, 171; of God (for man), *xv,* 5, 13, 36, 42–43, 123; of one's neighbor, 36, 38, 39, 40, 44–45, 58, 75, 81, 98, 114, 120, 145–46, 165, 171; in praxis of noticing, 93–94, 96–101; role in decision making, 161–67, 169–70, 171

Lowith, Karl, 191n.1

Loyola. *See* Ignatius of Loyola

Lozano, J. M., 189n.8

Lucifer. *See* Satan

Luke (apostle), 95; Gospel of, 70–71, 74

Marechal, Joseph, 188n.7

Mark (apostle), 74; Gospel of, 72–73, 105, 120, 160

Martha (biblical figure), 69, 92

Martyrdom, early Christians, 106

Marx, Karl, 20, 76, 113

Marxism, 28

Mary, Virgin, 69, 109; Motherhood of, 52

Mary Magdalene (biblical figure), 69

Massage, technique of, 26

Materialism, secular, 77

Matthew (apostle), 37, 70, 90, 155; Gospel of, 49, 67, 74

Meaning, question of, 104, 116–17, 129

Meditation, 30, *diagram,* 31, 104–24, 131, 143, 150; ascensional, 108–9, 124, 143; vs. contemplation, 104, 125, 128, 134; defined, 104, 111, 116, 117; goal of, 134; history of, 104–11; prechoice and postchoice purposes of, 120–24,

143; questions for, 112–15, 116–
17; return phase, 124, 143, 172,
173–74, 175–76; style of, 115–16;
technique, 107–8, 109; and un-
derstanding, 117–19, 121, 127;
writing down, 105–7
*Metanoia*, 3
Middle Ages, 107–8
Misery, 44
Models, 62–63; relativity of, 63
Moltmann, Jürgen, 189n.11
Monasticism, 106–7, 109
Montague, George, 187n.2(ch.4)
Mood, taint of, 98–99, 123
Moral fear, 157, 160–61, 166–67,
171, 175, 178, 180
Moral impotence (frigidity), 157,
158–60, 161, 171, 175, 178, 180
Moral relativism, 157–58, 161,
171, 175, 178, 180
Moses, 90
Music, 36, 37
Myers-Briggs analysis, 27,
186n.4
Myths, questioning of, 21

Natural sciences, 76, 77, 81
Neo-orthodoxy, conservative, 49
Neoplatonism, 107, 110, 111
New Jerusalem, 58. *See also* City
of God
Newman, John Henry, 133–34, 135,
190ns.4, 6
New Testament. *See* Bible; Gospels
Newton, Sir Isaac, 64
Nicene Creed, *xvi*, 188n.1
Nicodemus, 68, 92, 109
*Night* (Wiesel), 35
Noticing, praxis of, 30, *diagram*,
31, 84–103, 112, 123, 127, 150;
of consolation and desolation,
96–102; as habit, 87–88; of inner
experience, 88–96; posing ques-
tions, 85–86; return phase of,
143, 172, 174–76

O'Connor, Flannery, 22
Old Testament. *See* Bible
*On the Christian Combat* (Saint
Augustine), 75
Origen, 51, 106, 108, 126

Pain, experience of, 92–93, 112
Palmer, Helen, 186n.4
Pannenberg, Wolfgang, 188n.1
Passion of Christ, 35, 73
Patterson, L. G., 188n.3
Paul (apostle), 53, 56, 75, 90, 95,
109, 110–11, 115, 158, 163, 164–
65, 189n.10
Pentecost, 67, 70–71
Person-in-community-in-history,
150, 161
Peter (apostle), 67, 71, 73, 92, 109,
115, 137–39
Pharisees, 67, 72
Philip (apostle), 95, 109
Picasso, Pablo, 35
Pius XII, Pope, 189n.13
Plato, 23, 37, 107, 126, 145
Platonism, 105, 108
Plotinus, 107, 125, 126, 144, 145,
188n.7
*Potato Eaters* (Van Gogh), 35
Praxis, spiritual, 14–16, 37; Circle
of, 30–31, *diagram*, 31, 124, 174;
defined, 14–15; discernment of
spirits, 16, 17–19, 21; discernment of stories, 21–22; handling
communal response, 24–26; liberation, 28–29; vs. practice, 14–
16; processes of, 30; vs. technique, 26–28, 116; tradition and,
22–24, 25–26. *See also* Contemplation; Deliberation; Meditation; Noticing
Prayer, 18, 27
Preservative image, 66–68, 69, 70,
74–75, 75, 76, 77, 78, 81–82,
113, 157

Process images, 61–63, 66–74. *See also* Dialectical image; Interruptive image; Preservative image; Progressive image

Progressive image, 69–71, 72, 74–75, 76–77, 78, 81–82, 113, 157–58

Property, preoccupation with, 47, 49

Psychoanalysis, 177, 178–79, 180; questions and limits of, 180

Ptolemaic cosmology, 76

Questions, questioning, 136–39; in counseling, 180; in decision making, 150, 170; of inner experiences, 88–89; in praxis of noticing, 85–86, 90–91, 112; in praxis of meditation, 111–15; in psychoanalysis, 180; in spiritual mentoring, 181

Real assent. *See* Assent

Realization, in contemplation, 124, 130–33, 137, 141–42, 143, 145

Redemption, 51, 52

Reign of God, 53, 54, 56–59, 104, 122, 163; defined, 56–57; work of, 60, 62, 144

Relationship(s): assessment of, 8–9, 12, 85, 86–87, 119, 121–22, 142–43, 149, 172; dialectical nature of, 65, 71; to God, 32–46, 53; to God, broken, 46–49; horizontal, 68; integration of, 9–10, 12, 119, 121, 122–23, 142–43, 149, 172–76; vertical, 68

Religion, outer vs. inner content of, 38

Responsibility, 79; abdicating, 82; individual and group, 81, 170; taking, 19, 27, 171. *See also* Choice; Decision

Resurrection, 69, 94, 163

Retreat: definitions of, *xiii–xvi*, 4,

7–8, 149; meaning of, 4

Ritual, 12, 114

Ruysbroeck, Jan van, 188n.7

Saints. *See under proper names of Saints*

Salvation, 42, 56, 58, 61, 173; dialectical image of, 74–75

Satan, 76, 187n.4(ch.4)

Scholasticism, Plotinian, 188n.7

Sectarianism, 81

Secularism, 76–78

Self-centeredness, 47, 48–49, 79, 81–82, 160; community vs. individual, 49, 78, 81, 102

Self-hate, 165

Self-image, 99, 101

Self-love, 101, 165

Senses, outer experience of, 88, 89, 91

Sermon on the Mount, 67; Beatitudes, 94

Severus, E. von, 188ns.4, 6

Sexism, Christian, 52

Sinfulness, 39–40, 46, 47–49, 58, 99, 166

Skepticism, 22, 166

Social consciousness, 102, 113–14

Social philosophies, 170–71

Socrates, 104

Solignac, A., 188ns.4, 6

Solomon, King, 82

Spirit of God, *xv–xvi*, 42, 53, 58, 69, 71, 75, 90, 91, 107, 110, 132, 171. *See also* Holy Spirit; Word of God

*Spiritual Exercises* (Saint Ignatius of Loyola), *xii, xiv*, 1, 137, 144, 173, 185n.1(intro), 187n.4(ch.4), 190n.6

*Spiritual Exercises for Today: A Contemporary Presentation of the Classic Spiritual Exercises of Ignatius Loyola* (Dunne), *xiii–xiv*, 15, 97, 144

Statistical kind of insight, 64, 65
Stephen, Saint, 95
*Steps of Humility, The* (Bernard of Clairvaux), 187n.4(ch.4)
Stoicism, 107, 110
Struggle, inner, 74, 75
Suffering: of Christ, sharing, 173; of innocent and poor, 34–36, 37, 39, 43
Superego, 155–57
Suso, Heinrich, 188n.7

Tauler, Johannes, 188n.7
Techniques, mechanical, 26–28
Teresa, Mother, 55, 68
Teresa of Avila, Saint, 108
Tertullian, 106
Texts, choice of, in retreat, 139
Thomas (apostle), 92
Torah, 75
Totalitarianism, 81
Tradition: formation and passing down of, 22–23, 26; questioning of, 20–21, 22–24, 25–26; reliance on, 23–24, 25–26, 154
Traditionalism, 22
Training, of spiritual mentors, 182
Trinity, the, 44, 111

Understanding, 117–19, 127, 131; in counseling, 177–78, 179, 180; in psychoanalysis, 177, 179, 180
Urbina, Fernando, 186n.3

Value judgment. *See* Judgment, of value
Van Gogh, Vincent, 35
Vanier, Jean, 68
Vatican II Council, 108, 112
Viviano, Benedict, 187n.4(ch.3)

Ward, J. Neville, 190n.2
Werner, abbot of St. Blase, 187n.4(ch.4)
Who? question about God, 36, 37, 41, 145
Why? question to God, 34–35, 37, 39–40, 132
Wiesel, Elie, 35
Will of God, 56; discerning, 16–17
Winter, Gibson, 189n.15
Word of God, *xv, xvi,* 38–46, 53–59, 75, 90, 109–10, 132, 134; historical Jesus as, *xv, xvi,* 39, 40–41, 44, 46, 137, 171; as history, 38–39, 41–42, 43, 44, 45, 53–56, 105, 106–7, 188n.1; inner, 11, 37, 41–43, 44, 46, 49, 56, 91, 136, 144, 171; outer, 11, 37–41, 43, 44, 46, 49, 56, 91, 136, 144, 171; as "truth," 188n.1

Yahweh, 71, 105
Yoga technique, 26